To Dan and N[...]
[...]rds
of the Author, and faithful members
and Deacon at Glenfawn Baptist Church.
    May the comments of the Author
and the documented facts reveal a
greater perception of religious and
historical truths.

                Louis F. Asher
                    wja

John Clarke (1609-1676)

Pioneer in American Medicine,
Democratic Ideals, and
Champion of Religious Liberty

by

Louis Franklin Asher, Ph. D.

DORRANCE PUBLISHING CO., INC.
PITTSBURGH, PENNSYLVANIA 15222

ISBN #0-8059-4040-5
Library of Congress Catalog Card Number 96-092735
Printed in the United States of America

First Printing

For information or to order additional books, please write:
Dorrance Publishing Co., Inc.
643 Smithfield Street
Pittsburgh, Pennsylvania 15222
U.S.A.

To my wife and family for their undying love

and encouragement which made the task

of writing this book much easier.

Contents

Portrait of Dr. John Clarke

Some have identified the portrait on the dust cover of this book as a likeness of Dr. John Clarke, early American pioneer in medicine, law, democracy and religious freedom. A photo of the original painting appeared on the cover of *The Hero of Aquidneck* by Wilbur Cheesman Nelson. Nelson believed the painting was that of Dr. Clarke. In the past, the portrait has been identified variously as that of Dr. Clarke, Roger Williams, or simply as "The Unknown Clergyman."

The original oil painting of the clergyman measures several square feet in size and hangs in the Redwood Library and Athenaeum at Newport, Rhode Island. The date on the painting is 1639. In 1927, Providence artist Wilfred Duphinney suggested that possibly the painting is a likeness of Roger Williams; he conjectured that the date on the painting may be wrong and should be 1659 instead. When the author viewed the painting in 1965, the library catalogue listed the date as 1659, but no one at the library seemed acquainted with its history.

Dutch painter Guilliam DeVille painted the portrait. It has been assumed, however, that no painter could have painted it in New England as early as 1639, although, as early as 1647, a portrait was made of Indian Chief Ninigret of Rhode Island, which in 1965 was housed in the Rhode Island Historical Society Library at Providence. Relative to the conjectured date of 1659, only Dr. Clarke was in England at that time; Williams had returned to Rhode Island earlier.

The following seem to be the known facts in identifying the portrait of the "Unknown Clergyman":

(1) It is the portrait of a clergyman.

(2) His hair length borders on long because it touches his shoulders. While pictures of Roger Williams show the same hair length, other than this, there appears to be no similarity between this likeness and other pictures of Williams.

(3) Since both Dr. Clarke and Williams opposed "long" hair, evidently, such length to them was not considered long.

(4) The date of the painting on the portrait is 1639. Neither Dr. Clarke nor Williams was in England during 1639. While both were there from 1651 to 1654, only Clarke remained in England until 1664.

(5) No person other than Dr. Clarke or Williams has been suggested as a likeness of the portrait, insofar as the author is aware.

(6) Other pictures of Williams show no likeness to the painting.

(7) One of Dr. Clarke's descendents identified the painting as bearing a resemblance to the Clarke features and lines.

In one of Roger Williams' letters, Williams cited a man who visited Rhode Island, whom Williams described as strange because he wore long hair extending down his back. Since Williams considered long hair on a man as strange, it seems that such a man would stand out in New England. Evidently shoulder-length hair was not considered long at that time.

Off and on for years, attempts were made to identify the early portrait. Even though conclusive evidence is indeed lacking, which demonstrates beyond doubt the portrait is that of Dr. John Clarke of Rhode Island, by and large opinions seem to favor Clarke. Based on available evidence, the author believes the portrait is probably that of Dr. John Clarke who had it painted sometime between 1651 and 1664, during Clarke's long stay in England. Since the author has found no conclusive disclaimer to the contrary, he chose to use a facsimile of the portrait to adorn this book.

Acknowledgements

The author wishes to express his appreciation to the late professor Emeritus Dr. Louis A.R. Yates of Bradley University, Peoria, Illinois, who first inspired him to do good research work and who wrote encouraging words toward this work. Also the author is grateful for the advisory assistance given him on his master's thesis titled "The Life and Letters of John Clarke (1609-1676)" in 1966 by Drs. Archie P. McDonald and James L. Nichols, both retired professors form Stephen F. Austin State University, Nacogdoches, Texas.

The author acknowledges his gratitude for the help he received from the following libraries and research centers: the Massachusetts Historical Society, Boston, Massachusetts; the Newport Historical Society; Redwood Library; the United Baptist John Clarke Memorial Church—all of above in Newport, Rhode Island; Rhode Island Historical Society; Providence Public Library; John Hay Library, Brown University; Rhode Island State House— all of above in Providence, Rhode Island; Eastern Baptist Theological Seminary, Philadelphia, Pennsylvania; and University Microfilm, Ann Arbor, Michigan.

Further the author wishes to express his indebtedness to the following British and Dutch sources and records offices: the British Museum, Corporation of London Records Office, Guildhall; Public Record Office, Chancery lane—all of above in London; King Edward VI School, Bury St. Edmonds, Suffolk County, England; Ipswich and East Suffolk Record Office, County Hall, Ipswich, Suffolk County; the Honourable Society of the Middle Temple; the Honourable Society of the Inner Temple; the Honourable Society of Gray's Inn; the Honourable Society of Lincoln's Inn—all of London; Miss Mary H. Flower, hired searcher of 2 Lammas Park Gardens, London, W5.; the University of Cambridge, Cambridge, England; and the University of Leyden (Senaat Universiteit te Leiden), Leyden, Holland.

The following offices and persons were very cooperative in supplying information or suggestions where materials bearing on Dr. Clarke may be located: the Office of Recorder of Deeds, Providence, Rhode Island; Central Criminal Court, Old Bailey, London; County Records Offices, Shire Hall, Bedford, England; Greater London Record Office (Middlesex Records), London; Record Office, House of Lords, London; and Andover Newton Theological School, Newton Centre, Massachusetts. A special thanks is given to Dr. William D. Metz of the University of Rhode Island and a former editor of the Phi Alpha Theta *Journal* for reading the earlier manuscript and offering helpful advice; also to Wilbur Nelson, Jr., son of the late Rev. Wilbur Cheesman Nelson and Vice President of the Rhode Island Hospital Trust Company for his encouragement and support offered toward this work and numerous others, including my oldest son, Michael—who supplied me with a computer and other aids—without whose encouragement this book probably would not have been possible.

Introduction

Every student of American history knows the importance of Roger Williams. The battle for religious freedom, which he courageously initiated in New England, has been unceasingly proclaimed. But somehow it has escaped the attention of students that Williams' singular contribution has eclipsed other equally outstanding figures. One of the most neglected of these personages was Dr. John Clarke, physician, minister, colonial patriot, and benefactor of seventeenth-century Rhode Island. A close friend and political associate of Williams, Dr. Clarke hurled the same bold challenge against the church-state principle of government for which Williams became famous. In contrast to Williams, however, Clarke came to America fully persuaded in this conviction. Yet in recognition, Clarke has been given less than token attention. Thus very little about him and his contributions have been duly noted. Even Clarke's contemporaries have provided too little information.

Basically this book is an expansion of a thesis: "The Life and Letters of John Clarke, Physician of Rhode Island, 1609–1676," which was originally submitted in partial fulfillment of the requirements for the degree of master of arts at Stephen F. Austin State University in Nacogdoches, Texas, in 1966.

My thesis in this work is that John Clarke of Rhode Island was the initiator of democratic ideals in New England, he was an explorer in New England medicine, and he played a seminal role in establishing religious freedom in the Rhode Island colony by initiating it and legally upholding its practice.

The objective of this work aims at installing Dr. Clarke to his rightful place in history by rescuing him from historical oblivion. The methodology is by analyzing and evaluating his role in colonial America through an examination of his correspondences, his book, various university and Rhode Island State Records, contemporary letters and works—especially those which oppose his views, and all other materials that relate to him.

Several things can account for Clarke's obvious obscurity in history. Because of his common name, historical confusion is understandable. Yet his public life in Rhode Island appears to be well documented. In view of this, why has such a distinguished person been so callously ignored by historians, especially those in political science? The intellectual community, in fact, seems to be inadequately informed on the significant role of Clarke in formative America. As it happens, certain important ideals have been attributed to Roger Williams—such as the innovation of the "lively experiment" of democracy—which belong to Clarke.

Such obscurity aroused my curiosity and fired my enthusiasm to investigate further into the life and contributions of Clarke. In turn this led to a second research tour in New England, a lengthy correspondence of inquiries, and a tour to England in 1975. After serious reflection and examination of the materials relating to Clarke's era, I found several apparent reasons for Clarke's relative insignificance.

As a modest person, Clarke wrote very little about himself. A practical man, his prolific talents kept him occupied, affording him little time to write of personal matters. According to state records, matters of early colonial expediency kept Clarke very busy, and documents of historical importance were too often scribbled on loose pages; consequently they were not guarded very carefully. As a result, many valuable materials were either misplaced or destroyed. Along with these, many valuable papers and records were confiscated by British troops when they occupied the town of Newport during the War of Independence. To make matters worse, the ship which carried the confiscated records to England was lost; only a small box of papers was salvaged.

Unfortunately Clarke's relatively common name has caused considerable confusion in both England and New England. Now, however, Dr. Clarke of Rhode Island can be identified quite accurately. Finally, and perhaps more importantly, Clarke left no descendents to carry on his interests. Of his five brothers and sisters who migrated to America, only his brother Joseph continued the family name. Therefore no relative survived to make us aware and keep us informed on personal matters relating to Clarke.

Except for a few articles about Clarke, to author, little if anything of a secondary nature concerning Dr. Clarke has appeared in print for some three decades. Of course as late as 1975, two more of Clarke's personal letters were discovered in England. The letters are of a religious nature, and they merely confirm what this work states: Clarke as a minister served his religious brethren some while he was in England from 1651 to 1664.

Except for a few articles about Clarke, the few available secondary materials which relate to him span a number of years. To the author's knowledge, only two books, a dissertation and a master's thesis, have been composed on Clarke: *The Story of Dr. John Clarke* in 1915, by Thomas Williams Bickness; *The Hero of Aquidneck* in 1938, by Wilbur Cheesman Nelson; "John Clarke, Baptist Statesman," a Th.D. dissertation in 1950, by James Hallett Christian; and "The Life and Letters of John Clarke, Physician of Rhode

Island, 1609-1676," an M.A. thesis in 1966, by the author.

None of the above works has brought due recognition to Clarke. The books are not adequately documented, and the dissertation—although expertly documented—focuses mostly on the charter acquisition and its implications; little attention is paid to Clarke's other contributions. Although the thesis brings together more of Clarke's letters and other valid evidences, which bear on his diversified life, the thesis is basically more of a collection of source materials than a balanced interpretive work. However the thesis does make a serious attempt to identify the five or more John Clarkes that appeared in new England up to 1650.

None of the above four works explores in depth Clarke's religious views. Only a few of his letters relating to matters of state are examined, and insufficient attention is given to Clarke's education background. In general no documented narrative has been produced that presents a satisfactory, balanced assessment of Clarke's life, activities, and overall contributions to American society in New England. Therefore this book attempts to shed more light on Clarke's social, political, and religious role in helping to develop the infant American republic.

In the pioneer social context, John Clarke of Rhode Island contributed significantly to the medical, political, and religious developments of New England at large and the Rhode Island colony in particular. As a physician, Dr. Clarke made medical history by his extraction of a hydatdiform mole, the first in New England history. In this contribution, he is deserving of signal honor for his unselfish medical services to the Antinomian social outcasts of Massachusetts. Socially Clarke led out and helped found a distinctively unique colony in the New World when he helped transform a group of immigrant dissidents into an experimental democracy.

As the most forward and stable-minded man in the Antinomian camp, Clarke initiated the Rhode Island migration. Serving on the purchasing committee, he was in the initial founding group. As new towns sprang up and a growing concern for unity emerged, Clarke was chosen to lead the way. Helping to unite the towns, Clarke worked faithfully by assisting in framing, codifying, and executing the early laws of the unpopular colony. But more importantly, he was the principal author and acquirer of Rhode Island's famous civil and religious charter of freedom—the first of its kind in the world. As the chief instrument in drawing up the novel document, Clarke was then chosen to help lead the struggling colony toward an effective popular government.

Freedom of religion to many is the fountainhead from which all other freedoms flow. It has proved central to the democratic system, and ideal which has manifested to the world unique civil and religious liberties. While Roger Williams has been hailed as the earliest American harbinger of religious freedom, it was Dr. Clarke who activated the principle by making it the wellspring of democracy in early Rhode Island government. By implementing his pioneer democratic philosophy and religious liberty, Clarke made clear that the state is not to be used as an instrument of rule, a disciplinary agent—or even a guide to regulate religious matters.

In contrast to Williams, Clarke structured and helped to stabilize an infant republic, which became a role model for modern American democracy. Clarke steered the colony toward a government of unprecedented civil and religious liberty, convinced that otherwise a populace inevitably ends up subservient to the very wishes and whims of self-centered and overly ambitious rulers. At the first settlement of Portsmouth, for instance, such a direction was threatened by the Antinomians, and later at Newport by the usurping authority of Governor William Coddington and his immediate followers. Of course not all of Clarke's associates—such as the Puritans of New England at large—agreed with Clarke's democratic philosophy. To them free-spirited idealism too often fractures or veers off into anarchic tendencies, which at the outset became apparent. Such a threat was real to the Puritans; in fact it caused serious difficulties for some time between Rhode Island and the rest of New England.

Chapter 1
Quest for Identity

In Newport, Rhode Island, less than five blocks from the town square, a small cemetery plot contains the remains of a man whose memory has been all but obliterated by the exploits of his more illustrious contemporaries. The modest graves are set off from adjacent buildings and the main thoroughfare by a low cobblestone fence and are hardly noticed by passersby. Flanked on his right by his first wife, Elizabeth, on his left by his second wife, Jane, Dr. John Clarke, seventeenth-century physician, colonial statesman, Baptist minister, and author, lies amidst the noise and confusion of the modern city of Newport.

Located on what is now West Broadway, near the corner of Callender Avenue, the cemetery ground was originally part of a larger tract that belonged to Clarke. On the day of his death, he bequeathed the land to the church which he founded. His will assignment states:

> WHEREAS I, John Clarke of Newport, on Rhode Island, Physician...give and bequeath a small piece of land att the southeast corner of my orchard in the said town of Newport, unto William Weeden, Philip Smith and Richard Bailey and their heirs and assigns forever, for the use and uses to be by me declared under my hand and seal...so that they shall be seized thereof only for the use and behoof that Church of Christ on Rhode Island, unto which I am so nearly related for them and their successors to improve as a place for burial or for any other use for the said church as they shall have occasion.[1]

The common name of John Clarke has created considerable confusion, causing Clarke to be inaccurately identified by unwitting writers. Even the noted eighteenth-century Baptist historian Isaac Backus confused him with another Clarke who, Backus claimed, was disarmed in Boston in 1653.[2] Although a John Clarke was disarmed sometime later, his occupation was listed as farmer.[3] Moreover John Clarke, physician, according to his own account, did not arrive at Boston until November of 1637, two years after the date in which the Clarke whom Backus reported as disarmed.[4] Such a dilemma is due to the lack of precise information on the several Clarkes of that New England period.[5]

At least five men by the name of John Clark(e) are noted in New England during the years 1630 to 1664. John Clarke of Plymouth was a Lieutenant Colonel. His military correspondence contains a wealth of data on matters of British colonial interest, and he needs to be explored further.[6] Another

Clarke is cited only by name, his place of origin, and his time of migration.[7] A third one was a farmer who seems to have been the one who was disarmed. Professor and author Emery John Battis identifies this latter Clarke with the "peripheral group" of the Antinomians, whereas Dr. Clarke was among the personnel of the "support group."[8]

The farmer is cited several times in Governor John Winthrop's papers. His name appears in a letter on October 24, 1633, from Winthrop to his son John Jr. in which Winthrop acknowledged that he had word of his son by a "Mr. Clerke."[9] Further correspondence to his son on December 12, 1634, makes reference, presumably, to the same Clarke. Here he speaks of a "Mr. Clerke" who was dissatisfied with two of the servants, "John and Sarah," both of whom belonged to Winthrop, Jr.[10] A Clarke is cited in three other places in the Winthrop Papers. One is in a letter from "John Spenser to John Winthrop," dated April 1635. Again the context indicates this is the same "Clerke" as cited above.[11]

Because of the dates and contents of the letters, the two other places in which the name Clarke appears shed considerable light on distinguishing the farmer Clark from Dr. Clarke of Rhode Island. During the same month of Dr. Clarke's arrival, a John Clarke signed a document of apology, called the Wheelwright Petition, in which the signer acknowledged his obedience to the Massachusetts government as one which he confessed to be ordained of God. The date given for the signing of this apology was about November 22, 1637.[12]

It has been suggested that Dr. Clarke was among those disarmed. Although the time coincides with Dr. Clarke's presence in Massachusetts, the apology is not consistent with his speedy action to leave the colony. Nonetheless, in the Massachusetts records, as cited by editor James Savage, the Clarke who was disarmed in November 1637 was not Dr. Clarke, even though the Clark in question was among those later associates of Dr. Clarke in Rhode Island.[13]

Quite probably the Clarke who signed the document of apology was the disarmed farmer. Indeed this view is supported by Battis who is confident that the farmer was the only Clarke disarmed. Battis argues that neither Clarke nor any other of the three men who arrived at Boston with Dr. Clarke signed the Wheelwright Petition. The other three were Samuel Hutchinson, Stephen Greensmith, and Thomas Wilson.[14]

Therefore since no record exists that links Dr. Clarke the physician and minister—who arrived in Boston during November 1637—with those who remained in Massachusetts and had subsequent affiliations with the Puritans, it seems quite certain that Dr. Clarke did not have a personal confrontation at that early period with the Puritan oligarchy either politically or religiously.

Two other Clarkes appear in the records, and both were physicians: John Clark of Newbury and Boston and Dr. Clarke of Rhode Island. The former was a barber-surgeon, born in England sometime during the year 1598.[15]

According to a family tradition, as noted by James Thacher, this Clark held a diploma as barber-surgeon with which he was honored "for his success in cutting for the stone." This Clark migrated to Massachusetts in July 1634. His will bequeathed to his son (also named John) such items as "mares and horses, gold, silver, books, and several chirurgery instruments, medicines, drugs, and a pocket watch."[16] On one occasion, Roger Williams tells us that his wife took their daughter, Mary, to this Clarke whom Williams cites as "Mr. Clarke of Boston." Further he is presented in the Winthrop Papers as "Dr. John Clarke, physician of Newbury and Boston, who died in January 1644–5."[17]

Regrettably the other Dr. Clarke of New England—the subject of this work—is very difficult to identify merely by the early Massachusetts records. At any rate, during this period only one John Clarke cited in the Winthrop Papers is listed as a minister. Sir Barnardiston wrote John Winthrop on April 4, 1637, expressing his concern that he had not heard from him, even though he sent a letter to him "by Mr. Clarke a minister," who he understood had "safely arrived with Mr. Rogers."[18]

Granting that this was Dr. Clarke who removed to Rhode Island almost immediately upon his arrival at Boston in November of 1637, this appears to be the first suggestion of a direct relationship between him and the Puritans of Massachusetts. Was Barnardiston misinformed or did he refer to Dr. Clarke, who—for some reason not yet known to us—was detained until November? To be sure, granting the latter conjecture, Dr. Clarke could have undergone a religious change during the time in question, which would then explain his opposition of the Massachusetts Puritans from the moment of his arrival. Unfortunately Barnardiston fails to offer further help in solving the riddle, and Dr. Clarke says nothing that would help clear up the matter.

According to editor James Savage, Winthrop wrote of the arrival of a Mr. Rogers the previous year, but, as the following account states, no reference was made of a minister named Clarke:

> Two ships arrived here from London, and one a week before. They were full of passengers,—men, women and children. One of them had been from London twenty-six weeks, and between land and land eighteen weeks; (the other two something less time;) their beer all spent and leaked out a month before their arrival, so as they were forced to stinking water (and that very little) mixt with sack or vinegar, and their other provisions very short and bad. Yet, through the great providence of the Lord, they came all safe on shore, and most of them sound, and well liking…There were aboard that ship two godly ministers, Mr. Nathaniel Rogers and Mr. Partridge.[19]

Granting that the above was the Rogers whom Barnardiston cited, no one has identified the Clarke whom he meant, unless it was Dr. Clarke of Rhode Island—whose location at this point raises further questions.

Unfortunately Dr. Clarke failed to shed any light on the matter. Of course it is conceivable that something detained Clarke or even he changed his original plans without informing his friend.

By conjecturing that Dr. Clarke underwent a change in religious persuasion during this period (as did Presbyterian Elder Hanserd Knollys), this would explain why Governor Winthrop treated Dr. Clarke so coldly by ignoring his arrival at Boston in the records and in his future hostile treatment and arrest of Dr. Clarke. After all this suggests that Dr. Clarke did not have the same cordial relationship with Winthrop and the Puritans as suggested by Sir Barnardiston in his letter to Governor Winthrop. This can be observed later in their adversarial political and religious relations. What seems more important, why did not Governor Winthrop bring out Clarke's radical change in religious persuasion from Puritan to Baptist—as he did with Obadiah Holmes—if such did occur? In any event, the identity of the minister Clarke, who was cited earlier by Barnardiston, has not been made satisfactorily.

Relatively little was known of Dr. Clarke's English background until the present century. Born in the country parish of Westhorpe, Suffolk County, England, on October 3, 1609,[20] Clarke was baptized in the local parish on October 8, 1609.[21] He was the third son and sixth child of a family of eight, whose father and mother were Thomas and Rose (Kerrich) Clarke. Dr. Clarke's ancestors were of "prosperous yeoman" stock who originally lived at Finningham, the adjacent parish to Westhorpe on the northeast. Clarke's grandfather John "established himself at Westhorpe after his marriage with Katherine Cooke of that parish."[22]

Aside from these scanty scraps of data, very little helpful information has appeared that reveals the activities of Dr. Clarke's early youth and English background. Numerous leads over a period of some thirty years have been followed; unfortunately little information has been received. A more satisfactory identity seems to have become blurred or even lost within the apparently inextricable maze of John Clark(e)s of seventeenth-century England. Although Dr. Clarke can now be distinguished more accurately from the John Clark(e)s of earliest New England history, much valuable insight relative to his activities in his native England still remains obscured.

CHAPTER I ENDNOTES

1. John Clarke, *Last Will and Testament*, 9–10. Drawn up on April 20, 1676, and "recorded in the Town Clerk's Office, of Middletown, R.I., in the Probate Records, in Book No. 3, on page 248, et seq." [sic]
   Copied by permission from a certified typewritten copy furnished by the Newport Historical Society. Hereafter cited as Clarke, Will.

2. Isaac Backus, *A History of New England with Particular Reference to the Denomination of Christians Called Baptists* (2 vols., Newton, Mass: Published by the Backus Historical Society, 1871), I, 70–71. Hereafter cited as Backus, *History of the Baptists*.

3. Emery John Battis, *Saints and Sectaries* (Chapel Hill, N.C.: The Univ. of North Carolina Press, 1962), 318, 323.

4. John Clarke, *Ill Newes from New-England: or a Narative of New-Englands Persecution…Also four conclusions touching the faith and order of the Gospel of Christ out of his last Will and Testament, confirmed and justified* (London: Printed by Henry Hills, 1652), 23.
   Copied by permission from Xerox furnished by Xerox Corporation, Ann Arbor, Michigan. In his book, Dr. Clarke spells his name both with and without the "e." More often than not, the name appears

as Clarke. Thus, in order to avoid confusion, the name will be cited hereafter as Clarke, and the above book will be cited as *Ill Newes*. Original pagination of book is confusing, so the author uses his numbering of pages throughout this work by counting from page 1.

5. Battis, *Saints and Sectaries*, 312–13, 323, 332. Professor Battis has helped clear up some of this confusion.

6. Great Britain, Public Record Office, *Calendar of State Papers, Colonial Series, America and the West Indies, 1574–1660*, 454. The entry dated May 13, 1656, gives Clarke's rank and discusses matters relative to pensions.

7. Charles Edward Banks, *The Planters of the Commonwealth* (Boston: Riverside Press, 1930), 117, 121. This Clark, whose name Battis spells without the "e," was not associated in any way with the Antinomians. Cf. *Battis, Saints and Sectaries*, 332.

8. Battis, *Saints and Sectaries*, 323.

9. *Winthrop Papers* (5 Vols., Boston, 1929–47) III:140.

10. The matter dealt with their servitude; the account indicates that this Clark was a farmer; cf. *Winthrop Papers* III:176–77.

11. Ibid., 196. John Spenser came to Ipswich in 1634. He became a freeman of the colony on September 3, 1634, and later removed to Newbury. His name frequently appears in the General Court records as a representative, both for Ipswich and Newbury.

12. Ibid., 514. A note in the *Winthrop Papers* states that the apology was written in Governor Winthrop's handwriting; it appears in the following words: "We acknowledge it [the government] to be of God, and that we are bound to be subject therto while we live under it and that it were sinfull in us to resist the same, or to goe about by any violent course to stoppe the Course of Justice."

13. James Savage ed., *History of New England* by John Winthrop (2 vols., Boston: Printed by Phelps and Farnham, 1825) I:248. If this were Dr. Clarke, why did not Winthrop reprimand him for having previously violated their laws when Dr. Clarke was arrested in Massachusetts in 1651? On the other hand, Winthrop cited Obadiah Holmes, a preacher convert under Clarke, who himself had defected from the Congregationalists in 1649. Holmes became a Baptist in 1649, and in 1651, the Congregationalists under then-Governor of Massachusetts John Endicott took severe action against Holmes, as will be observed later in the work.

14. Battis, *Saints and Sectaries*, 312, 323.

15. According to Banks in *Planters of the Commonwealth*, 117, 121, Clark of Newbury, it seems, arrived in July 1634. Of course it is remotely possible that he was a different Clark. James Thacher conjectures that this Clark "arrived in America about the year 1650." *American Medical Biography* I:222. Apparently this is an error because Roger Williams wrote that his wife and daughter visited him for medical treatment in 1649. It is quite plausible that Clark of Newbury was the "well trained physician" whom Backus confused with Dr. Clarke of Rhode Island.

16. James Thacher, *American Medical Biography* I:222. Thomas J. Wertenbaker, *The First Americans, 1607–1690*, Arthur Schlesinger and Dixon Ryan Fox, eds, *A History of American Life* (New York: Macmillan Company, 1927) II:174. Wertenbaker errored when he quoted Thacher as saying that his Clark was the "first regularly educated physician in New England." What Thacher really said was "the name of John Clark has been, for a longer succession of years than any other in our country, distinguished in the ranks of medical practitioners."

17. John Russell Bartlett ed, *The Letters of Roger Williams;* In *The Complete Writings of Roger Williams* (7 vols., New York: Russell & Russell, 1963) VI:187–89.

18. *Winthrop Papers* III:385.

19. Savage, *History of New England* I:205–206.

20. G. Andrews Moriarty, "The Education of Dr. John Clarke," *Rhode Island History*, vol. 15 (April 1956) 42. Nearly all sources give Clarke's birth as October 8, 1609, but his Bible records his baptism on that date. The Bible is a 1608 Geneva Version, housed in the Rhode Island Historical Society Library at Providence. Granting the accuracy of these dates, Clarke's baptism at age five days indicates quite certainly that his parents were not Baptist.

21. Clarke Family *Bible*.

22. Moriarty, *The Ancestry of Dr. John Clarke of Newport, Rhode Island* (Boston: Spartan Press, 1921) 4–5. A bulletin of information reprinted from the article titled "Genealogical Research in England" and published in the *New England Historical and Genealogical Register*, October 1921.

Chapter II
Man of Letters

Dr. John Clarke of Rhode Island lived at a time of great literary achievements. While he may have been a brilliant figure in his own right, his peers have eclipsed him. Nonetheless some have esteemed him highly in both talents and learning. The earliest Rhode Island historian, John Callender, A.M., a scholar himself, called Dr. Clarke a "Man of Letters."[1] Now if he was the minister Clarke whom Sir Nathaniel Barnardiston cited, then also he was noted by Barnardiston as "my schollar," a medieval expression that was used in the sixteenth and seventeenth centuries to refer to a well-educated person.[2]

A laborious search has failed to discover precisely where Clarke acquired his early education. King Edward VI School, Bury St. Edmunds, was located about 12 miles from Westhorpe and within Clarke's district. Its registry lists several Clarkes but only surnames are given. The Headmaster of the school, R.W. Elliott, was unable to identify Dr. Clarke from the fragmentary and confusing records.[3] Although a search in the East Suffolk Record Office uncovered certain interesting leads for further search, subsequent efforts have proven of little value for further evaluation. However those who are most informed on early British education agree that quite conceivably Clarke attended Bury St. Edmunds.

A university education appears clearly indicated from known facts of Dr. Clarke's life, and those who have taken notice of his background activities have expressed this sentiment. Regarding his title of physician, the question has been raised relative to university training. Researcher G. Andrews Moriarty failed to find Clarke among the few Oxford University students of that time. Since Clarke's parents were probably Puritans, it is perhaps more reasonable to assume that he attended Cambridge University.

During the seventeenth century, Cambridge was a prominent Puritan stronghold, and it was only a short distance west of Suffolk County.[4] Since both Clarke's father and mother passed away close to the time that he would have matriculated in college, it does seem tenable that such close proximity of Cambridge would have been the logical choice for Clarke.

From 1615 to 1723, forty-two students named John Clarke matriculated at Cambridge University.[5] Among this number, thirty-five names are recorded as Clarke and seven as Clerke. The list is chronological and, obviously, all but some thirteen of the names can be set aside solely on the basis of dates and other known data given. Quite probably the ninth and eleventh entries refer to Dr. Clarke, which are given as follows:

CLARKE, JOHN. Matric. sizar from ST. CATHARINE'S, Easter, 1627; B.A. 1630–1.

CLARKE, JOHN. Adm. at CORPUS CHRISTI, 1631. Of Norwich. Perhaps B.A. from St. Catharine's, 1634.[6]

Since Cambridge and Oxford were the only two recognized schools in England where Dr. Clarke could have attended, it seems rather certain that Clarke acquired his B.A. at St. Catherine's, Cambridge. Moreover, since Dr. Clarke demonstrated expertise in law and theology, quite plausibly, after graduating from St. Catharine's in 1631, he would have entered Corpus Christi College to study law and/or to earn a masters degree. Indeed this accorded with the two Cambridge entries; the timing was right, and this course of action would have afforded Clarke ample time then to complete his formal training before pursuing medical studies in 1635.

Dr. Clarke's social standing, liberal religious ideas, and the knowledge that he was a physician have led writers interested in Clarke's life to believe that he studied medicine at Leyden University in Holland. Former Rhode Island University history professor William D. Metz concluded that because of Clarke's title of physician he must have attended Leyden.[7] Professor Metz characterized him as "one of the elite of England's medical men, for physicians alone were addressed as 'doctor,'" and, he further added, "they were gentlemen and scholars, usually practicing among the upper classes and concerned primarily with the diagnosis of disease and the prescription of remedies." Moreover he maintained that Dr. Clarke was the only physician in Boston when Clarke arrived in 1637.[8]

The different records which have been presented to show that Clarke studied medicine at Leyden are conflicting and confusing, to say the least. One of his biographers, Thomas Williams Bicknell—many years ago—wrote, emphatically, that Clarke obtained a medical degree at Leyden. He cited as evidence the following entry: "John Clarke, England 17 July, 1635–273. A catalogue of the Students of the Academy at Leyden, Batavia, 1575–1875."[9] Some five years after Bicknell's account appeared, Moriarty gave the same source as probably that of Dr. Clarke of Rhode Island.[10]

A much later attempt to locate Dr. Clarke at Leyden was made in 1950 by James Hallett Christian, but according to the Leyden University registry his source is faulty. In Christian's dissertation the source appears as follows: "John Clarke Leyden November 26, 1632, degree in medicine, Album Studiosorum Academiae Lugduno Batavae, MDLXXVMDCCCLXXV (Hagae Comitum apud Martinum Nijhoff, 1875), p. 240."[11]

The Leyden University librarian, P.C. Boren, maintained, "The printed *Album Studiosorum Acad. Lugd. Bat.* (The Hague 1875) doesn't give [sic] the text word by word," as Christian cited it above.[12] Further by a careful comparison with the official record two major errors are apparent between Christian's source and the one the librarian cited: the date of this Clarke's degree and his nationality, which is French. This becomes apparent from the cited record: "Archieven van Senaat en Faculteiten 9 (Volumen inscriptionum III), fol. 37r:

1631 Nov. 26. Johannes Clericus gallus Rothomagensis studiosus medicinae annorum XXIII, Habitat apud Thomam Bube."[13]

During the period from 1630 to 1664, only one John Clarke whose birthplace was listed as England studied medicine at Leyden, according to Boren, the Leyden University librarian. Enrolling in 1637, he took his degree on July 29, 1639; the school record appears in the following manner:

> 1637 Mart. 24. Joannes Clerck, Anglo-Britannus, annorum 23, studiosus medicinae, bij Nicholaum Moncq.
> 1639 Jun. 1. Joannes Clerck Anglus studiosus medicinae annorum 25. Habitat apud Wouter den Haen op den hoeck van de papengracht.[14]

Although Dr. Clarke's title of physician warrants a search for evidence of training apart from the two leading medical schools in Europe during the seventeenth century, Padua and Leyden, a concerted effort was made to discover and identify, if possible, all of the Clarkes of England at other schools. Following this method, only one interesting lead was disclosed. In England one John Clarke was "admitted to the freedom by servitude, having served his term of apprenticeship with George Dunn, surgeon, on September 24, 1635 (Guildhall Library, Ms. 5265/1, fol. 86v)."[15] Of course there is not at any time an association of Dr. Clarke with that of a surgeon.

Since surgeons were differentiated from practicing physicians by title, it seems quite certain that the above was not Dr. Clarke of Rhode Island. Researching this matter revealed considerable confusion in deciphering these ancient records. Still it seems more plausible to assume that Clarke studied at Leyden, and the more persistent parties of research have stated this strong probability. It must be noted, however, that errors have been made, perhaps on the part of past recorded administrative entries at the Leyden University or some records may have been lost. In fact the librarian even suggests this.[16]

Indeed the above conclusion appears to be corroborated by the research of Robert William Innes Smith, M.D., University of Edinburgh, who conducted a personal search of the Leyden records of all Englishmen who studied at Leyden.[17] In his research, Dr. Smith found that at least three Englishmen named John Clarke studied medicine at Leyden during the period under investigation. One of these names coincides with the one cited by both Bicknell and Moriarty. The listing is very brief and appears in the record entry as follows: "Clerk (Clarcq) Johannes. Anglus, July 17, 1635, aet. 21. Med."[18]

Assuming that Dr. Clarke attended Leyden and returned to England, evidence appears lacking to show that he became a Fellow or Licentiate of the Royal College of Physicians. Munck's *Roll* of names for the college lists only two John Clarkes at that time, neither of whom is Dr. Clarke. Rather they are father and son.[19]

In the seventeenth century there were no formal members of the college as such, only "Fellows and Licentiates," according to the librarian at the Royal College of Physicians. He claimed,

Licentiates were required to undergo an examination for their license to practice, and without it were liable to prosecution by the College, especially if they practiced in London and within a radius of 7 miles. Candidates for the Fellowship also had to undergo an examination, although occasionally Fellows might be elected without. Furthermore, those aspiring to Fellowship had to be graduates of either Oxford or Cambridge, or incorporated at one of these universities on the basis of a foreign medical qualification.[20]

L.M. Payne of the Royal College of Physicians evidences that there is no record in the "Annals" indicating that proceedings were taken against a John Clarke for practicing medicine without a license. Because of this, Payne feels, either Clarke was a licensed physician or he did not practice medicine to any extent while he was in London.[21]

Because of the confusing and incomplete records, it becomes difficult to evaluate accurately Clarke's medical training and practice outside of New England. A persistent effort to locate any record of Clarke's license has yielded virtually nothing, but in view of the watchdog surveillance of the Royal College of Physicians, it seems quite plausible that legal censure would be evidenced against Dr. Clarke had he not been duly licensed.

Inasmuch as three interested writers, Bicknell, Moriarty, and Dr. Smith, concur in their findings, and since the Leyden librarian can neither disallow nor offer a satisfactory explanation for the record of Dr. Clarke's medical degree, it remains quite conceivable that Clarke studied medicine at Leyden.

In the author's first inquiry to Leyden University, the librarian said the present records list only one Englishman named John Clarke who studied at Leyden (in any area of study) during the period in question. Persistent inquiries, however, yielded more fruit. Evidently the basis for locating a graduate was by his thesis. Since, apparently, none was filed there by Dr. Clarke, the librarian assumed he never obtained his degree there. Yet later he wrote that some of those who are accredited with having taken degrees there, also, left no thesis copies on file. Some may have been filed elsewhere, of course, or they may have been lost, as the librarian suggested.[22]

As it happens, Dr. Clarke's journey from Leyden, as yet, has not been documented. On the one hand, it appears that he was not a Fellow of the Royal College of Physicians, nor is there a record of another Clarke from England at this particular time who took a degree—or even studied medicine at Leyden—and then returned to England to live. On the other hand, granting that Clarke received a medical degree at Leyden in 1637, he would have had very little time to tarry in England before embarking for Boston in the New World, in order for him to arrive there by November 1637.

By Clarke's own statement, it seems certain that he did not leave for Boston directly from Holland. But, again, he could have returned to England and remained there until August before sailing for New England. It so happens that Chirurgeon John Clark of Newbury made the trip from April to

July of 1634.[23] Such a short stay in England, then, would account for Dr. Clarke's non-association with the Royal College of Physicians.

To be sure, Dr. Clarke's medical skill demonstrated formal training, and not one of his peers denigrated his educational background. His medical practice in fact is corroborated by the known facts relating to his life in New England and Old England itself. In his book, *Ill Newes*, he wrote the title of physician after his name.[24] Others assigned the title to him. Governor Winthrop of Massachusetts wrote in his *Journal*, sometime between September 7 and 21 of 1638, that Clarke was "a physician and a preacher to those of the island;"[25] if indeed Dr. Clarke's medical training were questionable, Winthrop would no doubt have noted it.

Credible evidence of Clarke's medical practice in fact has been documented, and we are indebted to the Puritans for supplying us with the few accounts, apparently extant. Such notations have provided invaluable testimony to otherwise unrecorded or lost information. An excellent example of this appeared in the medical attention that Dr. Clarke rendered to the notorious Anne Hutchinson.

A letter from Dr. Clarke to Governor Winthrop, penned sometime in 1638, documents Clarke as the attending physician to Anne before she removed from Rhode Island. Winthrop cites Clarke's service in clear detail. Dr. Clarke wrote,

> He was sent for several times and that he considered her condition both doubtful and dangerous. He was somewhat unwilling to meddle, at least before her delivery, but only advised to procure some medicines from the bay proper for the occasion...I conceived if it were a child, it was dead, but rather that it was not, but such a thing was afterward it proved.[26]

Dr. Clarke's preliminary diagnosis, then, was that it was not a pregnancy, and his medical observations and subsequent service to Anne Hutchinson, it would seem, should have silenced the rumor that she gave birth to a "monstrous creature." Since Anne had been expelled from Massachusetts by an intolerant New England clergy, a deformed offspring would substantiate the wild claims and their judgmental posture and, in turn, confirm their action as a just one.

As it turned out, of course, Clarke by his medical treatment of the matter dispelled such irrational notion. It was not a fetus at all but a rare medical phenomenon, unknown in New England at that early date. Interestingly modern medical science has credited Dr. Clarke with having extracted the first case of Hydatidiform Mole in recorded New England history.[27]

The particulars of this unique exploratory accomplishment, analyzed and described in detail in a letter to Governor Winthrop, appeared in James Savage's edited account of the *Winthrop Papers*, as follows:

> Mrs. Hutchinson, six weeks before her delivery, perceived her body

to be greatly distempered, and her spirits failing, and in that regard doubtful of her life, as he sent to me, &c. and not long after (in *immoderate fluor* and urine)[28] it was brought to light, and I was called to see it, where I beheld first unwashed, (and afterwards in warm water,) several lumps, every one of them greatly confused, and if you consider each of them according to the representation of the whole, they were altogether without form; but if they were considered in respect of the parts of each lump of flesh, then there was a representation of innumerable distinct bodies in the form of a globe, not much unlike the swims of some fish, so confusedly knit together by so many several strings, (which I conceive were the beginning of veins and nerves,) so that it was impossible either to number the small round pieces in every lump, much less to discern from whence every string did fetch small globes. I likewise opened, and perceived the matter of them (setting aside the membrane in which they were involumed,) to be partly wind and partly water. Of these several lumps there were about twenty-six, according to their relation of those, who more narrowly searched into the number of them. I took notice of six or seven of some bigness; the two, which differed much from the rest both in matter and form; and the whole was like the lobe[29] of the liver, being similar and every where like itself. When I opened it, the matter seemed to be hard[30] congealed.

The lumps were twenty-six or twenty-seven, distinct and not joined together; there came no secundine after them; six of them were as great as his fist, and one was great as two fists; the rest each less than the other, and the smallest about the bigness of the top of his thumb. The globes were round things, included in the lumps, about the bigness of a small Indian bean, and like the pearl in a man's eye. The two lumps, which differed from the rest, were like liver or congealed blood, and had no small globes in them, as the rest had.[31]

Since the last paragraph to Dr. Clarke's letter did not appear in his reply to Winthrop, editor James Savage explained, "The governour, not satisfied with this relation, spake after with the said Mr. Clarke, who thus cleared all the doubts."[32]

John Eliot, the famous pioneer Indian missionary and Bible translator, brought an unconfirmed allegation against a certain John Clarke medical practitioner of Boston. Eliot claimed that a "Mr. Clarke" caused the death of a woman who joined the Antinomians. Eliot recorded the account in his church records, according to Dale Miller.[33]

The identity of the above physician is not certain, but probably it was the Clark of Newbury and Boston, the same physician to whom Roger Williams's wife took their daughter for treatment. This John Clark matched the identity who posed a religious problem to the Massachusetts magistrates and who was forced to sign the Wheelwright Petition in order to remain in Boston. Because of his short stay of three weeks in Boston, it seems unlikely that Dr. Clarke later of Rhode Island practiced medicine in Massachusetts. No one in fact ever suggested that he practiced medicine in Boston or Newbury at any time.

Dr. Clarke repeatedly advertised his medical profession by imprinting "physician" following his signature. In addition the Rhode Island records cited him as physician a number of times, even in colonial correspondences to Clarke during his long stay in England. Moreover Dr. Clarke publicly announced himself as a physician while in London.

In his response to Clarke's book *Ill Newes*, Puritan author and religious teacher at Lynn, Massachusetts, cited Clarke as "John Clark of Road-Iland, Physician" on the title pages of both sections of his own book, *Civil Magistrates Power...*

The British *State Papers* in the Public Record Office in London cited Dr. Clarke as a physician when the English Parliament issued publisher and parliament printer Henry Hills a license to publish Clarke's *Bible Concordance* in 1654.[34]

In a legacy left to Dr. Clarke's first wife, Elizabeth, by her deceased father—which Clarke signed on May 12, 1656—was signed by Dr. Clarke as "physician of London." A letter to Clarke by the Rhode Island commissioners on October 18, 1660, began with: "To our Trusty and well beloved friend and agent, Mr. John Clarke of Rhode-Island, Physician, now residing in London or Westminster."[35] Then on July 15, 1663, Clarke signed an Indenture at London, a mortgage document to Richard Deanne of Middlesex County in which Clarke was cited as "Physician John Clarke gent Agent..."[36] Finally, in the last act of his productive life, Dr. Clarke wrote his Last Will and Testament in which he penned "John Clarke...Physician."

Such voluminous evidence appears conclusive that Dr. Clarke was both recognized and honored as a physician from the time of his arrival in London and throughout his tenure as colonial agent, both in Old England and New England. Quite plausibly either Clarke practiced medicine while he was in London or at least advertised his profession as physician. Without doubt Dr. Clarke of Rhode Island was a distinguished physician; at no time, it seems, was his skilled training questioned.

Despite this inability to locate precisely where Clarke received his undergraduate work and medical training, it seems certain that he acquired a well-disciplined formal education. The records demonstrate his trained skills, which are not usually attributed to self-disciplines but to those of a highly trained background. Since Clarke's medical expertise has been established, at present, no further assessment seems warranted due to the scarcity of credible documents.

The earliest appearance of the title "doctor" applied to Clarke seems to have been penned by Baptist chronicler Morgan Edwards about the year 1771. At that time, Edwards cited him as "Rev. John Clark, M.D."[37] Beyond these observations, Dr. Clarke's medical career appears relatively unknown and until the last century scarcely acknowledged.

In addition to Dr. Clarke's medical profession, he evidenced a knowledge of law and judiciary procedure. During the seventeenth century, England boasted of four law schools of note: The Honourable Society of the Middle Temple, The Honourable Society of the Inner Temple, The Honourable Society of Gray's Inn, and The Honourable Society of Lincoln's Inn. Although several men named John Clark studied law at these schools during Dr. Clarke's early years, none seems to coincide with him.[38]

Nonetheless, during Clarke's long period of service from 1651 to 1663, he spent most of his time lobbying to acquire the Rhode Island Charter; in addition Clarke worked out of Gray's Inn as a legal counselor. The Under Treasurer of Lincoln's Inn wrote this author that Clarke was "a Barrister of the Honourable Society of Grays Inn."[39]

It has been suggested that Dr. Clarke possibly studied law outside of London or even outside of England. As it happens, Governor John Winthrop's son, John Jr., studied law at Trinity College, Dublin, Ireland in 1624. No evidence, however, has turned up to substantiate that Dr. Clarke studied law there. Of course Clarke could have simply read law under the tutelage of his father.

Toward the end of the nineteenth century, one of the most famous of Texas governors, James Edward Ferguson, attended neither college nor law school but studied law on his own initiative. For two years he worked on a farm during the day and read "Blackstone's Law" and legal cases at night. He was admitted to the Bar in 1897; later he was elected governor. Between him and his wife, the Fergusons dominated Texas politics for more than thirty years.[40]

Nothing but conjectural evidence exists for the above, but it was worth exploring further. Author and professor John C.C. Clarke in *The First Baptist Church in America* suggested that Dr. Clarke's father was an attorney.[41] Granting this Clarke could have obtained a good legal foundation from his father. Here, however, a further conflict emerges. His father died before Dr. Clarke's eighteenth birthday, which—along with Clarke's college work—afforded little time for any substantive training, it seems. The family Bible shows that "Thomas Clarke, the father of these children departed this life the 29 of July 1627."[42]

Regrettably, like Dr. Clarke's other formal schooling, direct testimony that points to any formal training in law, apparently, has not been discovered. Further none of Clarke's contemporaries alluded to his educational background. On the other hand, Dr. Clarke was honored as an equal by his intellectual peers, whose formal educational training seems to be well documented. Clarke's many legal involvements, such as codifying Rhode Island laws, serving as English barrister, acting on behalf of Rhode Island in the British Parliament, drafting a unique charter, and serving in numerous other legal matters demonstrate that Clarke possessed considerable skill in legal matters, especially in view of the unquestioned ability of Clarke by his peers.[43]

In addition to medicine and law, Dr. Clarke was skilled in theology. His knowledge of the biblical languages of Greek and Hebrew and his awareness of certain theological issues of his day suggest formal training. But, again, all that can be learned about him is drawn from his own activities, contemporary testimony, and conjectural interpretations.

In Dr. Clarke's book *Ill Newes*, published in London in 1652, he evidenced a good knowledge of Scripture.[44] Moreover a biblical Concordance that he compiled was also published in England during Clarke's early tenure as agent for Rhode Island. A copy of the license to publish the Concordance was issued by the British Parliament on August 3, 1654:

> Order of the Council of State, John Clarke physician of Rhode Island, America, having composed and very closely compacted a new concordance to the Holy Scriptures of Truth, which in regard of its plainness & fullness, and yet smallness of volume & price, may prove singularly conducive to the help of those who desire to try all things in these trying times by that touchstone of truth, Henry Hills is licensed to print & publish the same, to the exclusion of all others, and the Company of Stationers are required to enter this order in their register.[45]

When Dr. Clarke drew up his will, he left the Concordance and all of his other books to his friend Richard Bailey, a witness to his will. The bequest reads, "Unto the said Richard Bailey I give and bequeath my Concordance and Lexicon to it belonging, written by myself, being the fruit of several years of study; my Hebrew Bibles, Buxtorff's and Passor's Lexicon, Cotton's Concordance and all the rest of my books."[46]

Although copies of Dr. Clarke's Concordance were circulated both in England and New England, no known copy has been located. Biographer Bicknell claimed the Harvard College Library contains an ancient book which he supposed may be an original copy. The inference, of course, seems too presumptuous because the publisher of this Clarke's Concordance was not Henry Hills.[47]

Whatever formal training that Dr. Clarke acquired, it seems evident that he obtained it before he arrived in the New World. Granting that he read law under his father, then attended Cambridge University from about 1627 to 1631 (or even before), Clarke would have had at least four years in which to study law further and/or theology before matriculating at Leyden in 1635. Two years at Leyden were sufficient for Clarke to receive his medical degree; he would then have had time to return to England and leave from there for America in time to arrive by November 1637.[48]

As it stands—at present—too much uncertainty enshrouds Dr. Clarke's educational background. Maintaining a low profile, he never wrote about his formal training and seldom mentioned his native past. Further we are without doubt certain that he has been confused with other John Clarkes, and in all probability, some of his materials have been lost among other records or unintentionally scattered. To be sure, some of the materials pursuant to colonial matters have been mixed with other John Clarkes.[49] This makes it very difficult to evaluate accurately Dr. Clarke's educational background; as a result, unfortunately a most significant phase of his life remains obscured.

CHAPTER II ENDNOTES

1. John Callender, *An Historical Discourse on the Civil and Religious Affairs of the Colony of Rhode Island and Providence Plantations in New England in America from the First Settlement 1638, to the End of the First Century* (Boston: Printed and Sold by S. Freelove and T. Green in Queen Street, 1739), p. 62. Hereafter cited as Callender, *Historical Discourse*. Callender obtained his M.A. degree at Harvard College and wrote the first history of the state of Rhode Island. The history often is called "Century Sermon."

2. *Winthrop Papers*, III, 212, 385.

3. Letter from R.W. Elliott, Headmaster, King Edward VI School, Bury St. Edmunds, County of Suffolk, England, to the author, August 29, 1965.

4. Moriarty, "Education of Dr. John Clarke," pp. 42–3.

5. Venn's *Alumni Cantabrigienses*, Part I, vol. I, 343.

6. Letter from Mary H. Flower, engaged searcher, 2 Lammas Park Gardens, London, W., England, to the author, March 2, 1966. It is possible, however, that Dr. Clarke received some of his education at one of the many Lollard educational institutions which flourished in and around Suffolk County during the sixteenth and seventeenth centuries. Many of the Lollard ministers were well trained in law, medicine, theology, and other of the arts and sciences. Because of the non-conformist stigma surrounding the Lollard Anabaptists, however, it seems very unlikely that public records were kept. On such schools, cf. John Foxe in his eight-volume work *Acts and Monuments*.

Although this conjecture may be worth exploring further, in view of known facts, it would seem very improbable. Like Dr. Clarke, Governor Winthrop came from Suffolk County, and he would have noted such non-conformity, it would seem.

7. William D. Metz, "John Clarke, Physician, Minister, and Statesman." This was an address delivered by Dr. Metz, professor of history at the dedication of the John Clarke Science Building at the Rhode Island College, July 8, 1963 (p. 3). Dr. Metz is a former editor of *The Historian: A Journal of History* published quarterly by the Phi Alpha Theta National Honor Society.

8. Ibid.

9. Thomas Williams Bicknell, *The Story of Dr. John Clarke*. The Founder of the First Free Commonwealth of the World on the Basis of "Full Liberty in Religious Concernments" (Providence: Published by the Author, 1915), p. 74.

10. Moriarty, "Education of Dr. John Clarke," p. 43.

11. Letter from P.C. Boeren, for the Librarian, Library of the University of Leyden (Bibliotheek der Rijksuniversiteit te Leiden), Leyden, Netherlands, to the author, January 10, 1966. James Hallett Christian, "John Clarke, Baptist Statesman" (unpublished Th.D. dissertation, Eastern Baptist Theological Seminary, 1950), p. 6. Since then a study of Dr. Clarke was conducted by the author: Louis Franklin Asher, "The Life and Letters of John Clarke, Physician of Rhode Island, 1609–1676" (unpublished M.A. thesis, Stephen F. Austin State College, 1966).

12. Ibid.

13. Ibid. Boeren states that this French student, although enrolled as a student in medicine, took his degree in law.

14. Ibid. Dr. Clarke was in Rhode Island by this time.

15. Letter from A.H. Hall, Librarian, City Record Office, The Corporation of London, Guildhall Library, London, EC2, England, to the author, March 14, 1966. Further leads suggested by Hall revealed only indirect evidence which served, substantially, to eliminate any tenable connection.

16. Robert William Innes Smith, *English-Speaking Students of Medicine at the University of Leyden* (Edinburgh: Univ. of Edinburgh, 1932). The manuscript notebook of Smith's published work is in the library of the Royal College of Physicians. Librarian L.M. Payne says that insofar as he is aware Smith "went to Leyden for the purposes of his book." Letter from L.M. Payne, Librarian, Royal College of Physicians, Regent's Park, London NW1, England, to author, June 9, 1966.

17. Ibid., p. 46. The apparent conflict in age (Clarke would have been twenty-six, not twenty-one, at matriculation), could very well be an error. As Moriarty suggests, the Leyden registry very often gave only an approximation of ages.

18. Letter from L.M. Payne, to author, March 18, 1966. The son was one of the Englishmen in the Leyden records, obtaining his M.D. July 29, 1639. His thesis is on file in the British Museum; cf. Smith,

English-Speaking Students of Medicine, p. 46. Relative to Fellows at the college, the clerk for the Superintendent of the British Museum stated, "The earliest list of members of the Royal College of Physicians for London is dated 1676." The clerk added, "This list includes a 'Dr. John Clarke' under 'Honorary Fellows'." Letter from Mary Pearce, for the Superintendent, The British Museum, London WC1, England, to author, September 30, 1965.

19. Ibid., June 9, 1966.

20. Ibid., March 18, 1966.

21. Perhaps some of the records have been lost—as the case at Padua University; cf. Smith, *English-Speaking Students of Medicine,* p. 46. Another author, Maurice Bear Gordon was convinced that Dr. Clarke studied both medicine and theology at Leyden; cf. Gordon, *Aesculapius Comes to the Colonies* (Ventnor, New Jersey, 1949), p. 248.

22. Letter from Boeyen to author, Mar. 18, 1966.

23. Banks, *Planters of the Commonwealth,* pp. 117, 121.

24. Clarke, *Ill Newes,* Title Page, *et passim.*

25. James Kendall Hosmer, ed., *Original Narratives of Early American History, Winthrop's Journal* "History of New England" 1630–1649, 2 vols. (New York: Charles Scribner's Sons, 1908) I:277. Hereafter cited as Winthrop's *Journal.*

26. Savage, *History of New England,* I:271–73.

27. Margaret V. Richardson and Arthur T. Hertzig, "New England's First Recorded Hydatidiform Mole," *The New England Journal of Medicine,* 260 (Boston, 1959) 544–45.

28. It is uncertain whether these are the exact Latin words in Clarke's letter because, in Savage's notes, this is the way they appear, but in the letter text—as cited by Savage—the words appear as follows: "*in immoderato fluore uterino.*" In any case, Clarke probably meant either or both an excessive flow of the uterus or urine.

29. This is blank in the copied letter, but Savage says "it is strange, that the word, which the governour leaves blank, is, plainly, 'lobe' in the original letter." Savage *History of New England* I:273.

30. Ibid. In Winthrop's copy of Clarke's letter, he wrote "blood" here, but Savage adds that it should read "hard."

31. Ibid. Savage claimed he had Clarke's original letter before him; the "author's transcription is sufficiently accurate, and nearly literal." It is unfortunate that these facts have not been accurately recorded in New England history and expressed as such in relevant literature.
Since the last paragraph to Dr. Clarke's letter did not appear in his reply to Winthrop, editor James Savage explained, "The governour, not satisfied with this relation, spake after with the said Mr. Clarke, who thus cleared all the doubts." Ibid.

32. Ibid.

33. Dale Miller, "Protestantism and Politics in Rhode Island: 1636–1657" (unpublished Ph.D. dissertation, The Univ. of Chicago, 1955), p. 46, footnote 2. Miller copied his information from "A Report of the Record Commissioners" (Boston, 1881) VI: 77.

34. Great Britain, Public Record Office, *Calendar of State Papers, Colonial Series, Relating to John Clarke, 1643–73, America and the West Indies, 1574–1660,* vol. CIII, 219. It seems strange the College of Physicians did not reprimand Dr. Clarke if he was not a licensed physician.

35. Callender, *Historical Discourse,* Appendix; In *Collections of the Rhode-Island Historical Society* (Providence: Knowles, Vose & Company, 1838) IV:210, 239–40. This record indicates Dr. Clarke as a physician in London.

36. John Clarke *Indenture.* Original manuscript is preserved at the Newport Historical Society, Newport, R.I. A photostat of the original was permitted through the courtesy of the Newport Historical Society. The reproduction was made by the process of a high-contrast negative by the John T. Hopf Photographic studio in Newport, which the author has. Richard Deanne was a fellow minister with Dr. Clarke in England.

37. Morgan Edwards, *Materials for a History of the Baptists in Rhode Island;* In *Collections of the Rhode Island Historical Society* (Providence: Hammond Angell & Co., 1867) VI: 326.

38. Letters, D.V.A. Sankey, Librarian and Keeper of the Records, The Honourable Society of the Middle Temple, London, to author, January 6, 1966; Sub-Treasure, Treasurer's Office, The Honourable Society of the Inner Temple, London, to author, December 24, 1965; B.W. Cocks, Librarian, Gray's Inn, London, to author, March 4, 1966-May 26, 1966.
Three John Clarkes studied at Gray's Inn during this period, but only one—even remotely—could be identified with Dr. Clarke. He studied law there from 1633–34, and his residence was Abudge, Essex. Of course it remains possible that this was Dr. Clarke. While the timing was right, librarian Cocks could not connect him with Dr. Clarke.

39. Letter from H.C.H. Fairchild, Under Treasurer, The Honourable Society of Lincoln's Inn, London,

England, to the author April 19, 1966. Follow-up letters to Under Treasurer Fairchild's claim that Dr. Clarke was a Barrister at Gray's Inn have elicited no further reply.

40. Ouida Wallace (Ferguson) Nalle, *The Fergusons of Texas or "Two Governors for the Price of One"* (San Antonio: The Naylor Company, 1946), pp. 18–20. As it turned out, James Edward Ferguson was not asked even one question in the examination for his Bar license to practice law.

41. John C.C. Clarke, "Dr. John Clarke, of Newport, R.I.," Samuel Adlam and James Robinson Graves, eds. *The First Baptist Church in America* (Texarkana, Ark.-Texas: Baptist Sunday School Committee, 1939), p. 54.

42. Clarke, *Bible*, Introductory material.

43. Later in the work this will be demonstrated, but Dr. Clark's legal training needs to be explored further.

44. Clarke, *Ill Newes, passim.* One section which relates Dr. Clarke's theology covers fifty pages.

45. Great Britain, *Calendar of State Papers, Colonial Series, Relating to John Clarke of Rhode Island, 1643–1673*, Vol. CIII, 219. Letter from Miss Mary H. Flower, London, to author, November 18, 1965. Researcher Miss Flower made a typewritten copy of the Parliament license which appears above.

46. Clarke, Will, p. 5.

47. Bicknell, *Story of Dr. John Clarke*, p. 75. Based on all records which author has examined, Dr. Clarke never signed master of arts to his name, which this John Clark did.

48. Letter from Payne, to the author, March 18, 1966. This allows from June to November to travel from the Netherlands to England and on to Massachusetts, in order to arrive there when Dr. Clarke said he did.

49. Letter from Miss Flower, engaged researcher, London, to the author, March 1966. In some of the Calendars, Miss Flower found Dr. Clarke was confused with the Clarke of Plymouth, who was a military man. She claims many letters of this Clarke deal with naval matters, but the cataloguing appears very confusing. Nonetheless John Clarke of Plymouth should be investigated further.

Chapter III
Religious Pluralism

Antinomianism stood at the opposite pole of Congregationalism, both politically and theologically. The anarchy of Antinomianism jarred the rigid oligarchy of the Massachusetts Bay Colony and threatened the early Puritan church-state structure. Very early in its establishment, the Massachusetts colony legislated both civil and religious obedience; the secular and ecclesiastical arms became inseparable. During the tenure of John Winthrop, the first governor of the colony, the torch of religious intolerance within a religious state was ignited in New England. Before any religious pluralism emerged, the colony of Massachusetts General Court ruled in 1631 that membership in a church of the Bay area was prerequisite to full rights of citizenship.

To an outsider, such a religious oligarchy posed a threatening church/state rule. It did just that in fact for Dr. John Clarke, who arrived in Boston during the height of the Antinomian crisis.[1] Since he allied himself with the minority group of Antinomians, he immediately became an enemy to the Puritan religious designs. As professor William D. Metz of the University of Rhode Island described Clarke, "Twenty-eight years old, six feet tall, in vigorous good health, possessed of an attractive personality, exceptionally well educate, [and] happily married," the New World posed a real challenge to the adventuresome English physician and minister.[2]

Even though Dr. Clarke's religious persuasion forced him to make a radical decision, he promptly followed his convictions, he claims, well aware that he would become a social outcast. Since he chose without hesitation or serious thought, his decision, of course, was motivated by strong social and religious scruples, all of which will be demonstrated below.

On September 3, 1635, the freedom harbinger Roger Williams was banished from the Massachusetts Bay Colony.[3] When the committee arrived to inform Williams of the court's disposition, Williams had already departed. In the opinion of librarian and editor Howard Millar Chapin, Williams left Salem before he was officially banished so as to evade seizure by Captain Underhill.[4]

Like Williams, Anne Hutchinson boldly proclaimed a kindred spirit of defiant independence. Her religious persuasion of Antinomianism was publicly denounced as heresy, and also she was banished officially from the Bay area in October 1636.[5]

At first these antagonistic beliefs of the Antinomians to the New England Congregationalists aroused only minor opposition; however soon the religious exclusivism of the Bay area revealed its repugnance of independent spirits and overtly defied them. The magistrates labeled those holding religious opinions contrary to the Congregational Puritans as lawless Antinomians. Unlike the Puritans, who were governed by a "covenant of works," who considered it their duty to manifest sanctification by the works of Old Testament Law,[6] the Antinomians felt they were not under the Old Testament dispensation but considered themselves under the New Testament "covenant of grace."

Itinerant Episcopal attorney Thomas Lechford, "of Clements Inne, in the County of Middlesex…" toured New England sometime between 1639 and 1640. He carefully observed colonial matters and recorded his observations on the climate of social, political, and religious opinions and activities throughout the area. Lechford perceived a religious intolerance within all colonies of New England except that of Rhode Island, which was in its formative colonial stage.[7]

WAS DR. JOHN CLARKE OF THE PURITAN FAITH?

The political/religious pressure became so restrictive on all immigrants to the Bay that the Honorable William P. Sheffield of Newport, Rhode Island, United States Senator in the late nineteenth century, said they were given only three weeks either to join one of the churches in the area or to leave the Bay area.[8] To Dr. Clarke, this was not religious freedom or even religious tolerance. After all he, along with certain others, came to America to get away from religious intolerance.

In turn, because of Dr. Clarke's immediate decision to oppose the Massachusetts religious mandate, it seems very doubtful that he was identified with either the Puritan or Plymouth Separatist faith. To the author, no documentary evidence has appeared which supports such a widely held claim; in fact no Puritan in England, Holland, or New England has connected Clarke to one of the Puritan churches. Interestingly both Clarke and Governor Winthrop migrated from the same county in England[9] and in keeping with the Winthrop practice of detailed recordings, it seems almost certain that if the Puritans of either England or Holland had notified Winthrop of Clarke's Puritan or Separatist faith, Winthrop would have noted it. Editor Savage pointed out that "Mr. Winthrop kept a Journal of every important occurrence, from his first embarking for America, in 1630, to the year 1644."[10]

Why Winthrop ignored Clarke until after Clarke arrived in America, in any event, is a good question. He was silent about Dr. Clarke altogether until after Clarke and his Antinomian associates settled on Rhode Island. Then Winthrop said nothing about Clarke's religious affiliations except to call Clarke "a physician and a preacher to those on the island."[11]

Evidently this silence regarding Clarke's church affiliation when he arrived in Boston was true only for Dr. Clarke. Subsequent migrating ministers, including those who defected from Puritanism, were not so discourteously ignored. Robert Lenthal was apparently a Puritan minister in England but became a Baptist after becoming acquainted with Clarke. Before Lenthal returned to England, he was associated with Clarke at Newport, Rhode Island. In addressing Lenthal, Winthrop wrote that he had a good reputation in England, but after he arrived in Boston he "drank in some of Mrs. Hutchinson's opinions, as of justification before faith, etc."[12]

Basically the Congregationalists comprised two groups. On the one hand, the Separatists or Pilgrims sought reformation of the Church of England by separating themselves from the church. Persecution then under Elizabeth I forced them to find refuge in Holland. Because of the climate and other circumstances, several of the Separatists as exiles from John Robinson's congregation at Leyden left the Netherlands and settled at Plymouth, Massachusetts in 1620.

On the other hand were the Puritans. They were also nonconformists, but they remained members of the Church of England while they sought to reform the church of her hierarchy, ceremonies, and certain other traditions. At the same time, of course, they continued to own the Anglican Church as the "Mother Church." Their principal settlement was in and near Boston in 1628. And by 1631, Congregationalism was firmly entrenched in Massachusetts; between 1635 and 1640, it was planted in the Connecticut Colony.

If Dr. Clarke was identified with the Congregational religious persuasion in the recent past, he failed to suggest it when he first arrived in Boston or even when he made contact with the Plymouth settlers a short time later. Moreover Governor Edward Winslow of the Plymouth Colony was a member of John Robinson's Separatist congregation for three years before migrating to New England, and he maintained a regular correspondence with Leyden. At no time—of which author is aware—did he suggest that Clarke was a member of the Separatist group in Leyden.[13]

It appears evident from Clarke's own confession that he was in no way committed either to the Puritan Congregationalists in Boston or the Separatists at Plymouth. At least he left this impression when upon his first contact with the Plymouth settlers he told them that his group wanted "to get cleer of all, and be of ourselves."[14]

It would still remain possible of course that the Clarke whom Barnardiston cited was Dr. Clarke of Rhode Island. If so when Barnardiston last heard form Clarke he was a Puritan minister, then later he became a Baptist. At least two men by the name of Rogers were closely acquainted with Winthrop, Ezekiel, and Nathaniel.[15] Nonetheless Dr. Clarke offered no hint that he had recently adopted Baptist opinions at the time they became obvious, at the latest, 1648.

In 1651 Clarke made public an expression of his beliefs. The first pronouncement of his religious convictions demonstrated his repugnance of the Puritan religious beliefs and intolerance. This was illustrated by both his liberal spirit of toleration and his own theological beliefs. While theologically they were strongly hostile to the Congregational Puritans, they were remarkable in harmony with the English Particular Baptists of London.[16]

As a Baptist, Clarke boldly exposed the intolerant, but widely acclaimed, Puritan church/state structure and publicly denounced their covenantal baptism as unfounded by the Scriptures. He unflinchingly charged the New England clergy as unbaptized and unordained usurpers of the true Christian ministry and maintained that their churches were improperly constituted and governed.

Unlike Roger Williams and his vacillating opinions in religious practices, Clarke opposed even the slightest compliance to the Puritan rule; that is mere attendance in one of their churches. Moreover Clarke never wavered from his Baptist convictions. Clarke's beliefs bore a kinship to the Antinomians but in a way which was both confusing and misleading to the Puritan magistracy. He did not share in the Antinomian religious notions altogether, but according to his own account, he opted to associate with the Antinomians for two basic reasons: He believed in the free exercise of the individual conscience, and he held to the basic premise of Antinomianism, a "covenant of grace."[17] Puritanism denounced both of these beliefs. Winthrop argued the covenant of grace was one of Mrs. Hutchinson's "errors." Further he denied that "the person of the Holy Ghost dwells in a justified person," and "no sanctification can help to evidence to us our justification."[18] The Puritans were very vocal against liberty of conscience; this will become apparent throughout this work.

Author Dale Miller classified Dr. Clarke as a "nomian." His list of classifications, as set forth by Jerald Brauer and borrowed by Miller, classified a nomian as one who holds to the infallibility of the Scriptures. Here Miller seems to have ignored Clarke's belief in the covenant of grace, a notion which Clarke never abandoned and one which Miller styled Evangelical. To be more accurate then, according to Miller's own classification Clarke should be characterized as a Nomian Evangelical.[19]

Confusion over the "Antinomian controversy would seem either due to Anne Hutchinson's nebulous concept of the latter part of the Antinomian premise or perhaps to her inability to explain her position intelligibly. This seems to be evidenced by Clarke's clear articulation on the point of controversy when he said,

> I was no sooner on shore, but there appeared to me differences among them touching the Covenants, and in point of evidencing a mans good estate, some prest hard for the covenant of works, and for sanctification to be the first and chief evidence, others prest as hard for the evidence of the Spirit, as that which is more certain, constant, and satisfactory witness...whereupon I moved the latter.[20]

By Clarke's bold expression of his religious conviction, he proclaimed his religious preference and stamped himself as a leader. From here on, the young physician and preacher, predisposed toward the freedom of individual conscience, displayed religious convictions antagonistic to those of the Bay, and by his bold initiative took on a new function. He became a leader and helper in colonizing a new settlement when his motion for relocating "was readily accepted." Along with others, Clarke was requested to search out a suitable place for a permanent settlement, to which he quickly assented, as indicated in his remark, "I was ready to do."[21] The migration was a history-making epoch; here was the formal beginning of a new state: Rhode Island.

Although it may be too presumptuous to say that Dr. Clarke was "the leader" among the social dissidents, it appears obvious from the earliest records that the Antinomian departure was activated by Clarke's initiative. He joined them, he moved for their relocation; in turn they appointed him (and certain others), of course, to make the forward step and explore the surrounding territory in search of a new land of settlement. Thereafter virtually each time an unprecedented move was needed, Clarke was appointed or elected to spearhead it.

Even before Anne Hutchinson was officially banished from Massachusetts, the Antinomian scouting party moved north in search of a place more to their liking. Because of the suffocating heat of the summer before, Clarke and the other members of his party explored the area near Exeter, New Hampshire. Here they encountered the other extreme of climate, and their dissatisfaction of the cold winters again moved them southward. According to Clarke, the party sailed to Providence, and there they were "courteously and lovingly received" by Roger Williams.[22]

THE FIRST RHODE ISLAND CHARTER

On March 7, 1638, the band of nineteen Antinomians assembled, presumably at Boston, and drew up a charter of government.[23] The compact was the first Rhode Island charter of government and came to be known as the "Portsmouth Compact." Since two major parts of the document are not in the records, authorship of the document remains uncertain.[24] However evidence of authorship points either to Clarke or William Aspinwall. Miller conjectures it was more likely Aspinwall because he retained his theocratic convictions, which Miller maintains is demonstrated by Aspinwall's later activity with the Fifth Monarchy movement in England. But Miller presumes that Clarke shifted his religious focus when he "moved away from theocracy by becoming a Baptist."[25]

The compact itself appears in the records as follows:

> The 7th day of the first month, 1638.
> We whose names are underwritten do here solemnly in the presence of Jehovah incorporate ourselves into a Bodie Politick and as he shall help, will submit our persons, lives and estates unto our Lord Jesus Christ, the King of Kings and Lord of Lords and to all these perfect and most absolute lawes of his given us in his holy word of truth, to be guided and judged thereby.[26]

The compact, to be sure, was a religious covenant and more on the order of a church covenant than a secular compact. Thus since Clarke was the only recognized minister among them, and the biblical references cited as support for the agreement were taken from Clarke's Bible, it seems more likely that Clarke wrote the compact. The passages marked in his Bible were Exodus 24:3, 4; II Chronicles 2:3; and II Kings 11:17.

During the effort of the Antinomian group to find a suitable permanent settlement, Anne Hutchinson was placed under house arrest. According to Winthrop, she was well provided for; because of the inclement weather she was allowed to remain in her home until the following spring.[27]

Following the failure of a final effort by the Massachusetts authorities to secure Anne Hutchinson's repentance, on March 22, 1638, she was ordered to leave the confines of the Massachusetts Bay by the last of the month. On March 28—four days after the deed for Aquidneck (Rhode Island) was signed and witnessed—Anne Hutchinson left Boston. First, she went to her farm at Mount Wollaston; from there she traveled by land to Providence.[28] By the time she arrived in Providence, the Antinomians under the aggressive and efficient support of Dr. Clarke, Coddington, William Hutchinson, and—as Chapin suggests—certain others had acquired legal ownership of their new home, the Island of Aquidneck, later known as Rhode Island.[29]

Thus under the inspiration and capable leadership of the young physician, minister, and now colonizer, Dr. John Clarke—lately arrived in the New World—a new frontier was opened. As it proved in time, this became a pioneer effort, which would soon put into effective practice the ground rules for a free society, and in particular a law granting religious tolerance that was so courageously heralded by the already noted religious and political nonconformist Roger Williams.

CHAPTER III ENDNOTES

1. Clarke, *Ill Newes*, 23, 24.

2. Metz, "John Clarke, Physician, Minister, and Statesman," p. 3.

3. Bartlett, *Letters of Roger Williams*, VI, 2, footnote.

4. Howard Millar Chapin, ed. *Documentary History of Rhode Island* (2 vols.; Providence: Preston and Rounds Co., 1916–1919) I:1. Chapin was librarian for the Rhode Island Historical Society. Hereafter cited as Chapin, *History of Rhode Island*.

5. Winthrop's *Journal*, I:195.

6. To the Antinomians, the Old Testament Law was not binding on Christians because they were under grace. To men of Dr. Clarke's persuasion, this meant that they were not bound by Old Testament Law because that was a covenant of works. To them and other Christians, salvation as taught in the New Testament comes through grace. Cf. Joseph Henry Thayer, *Greek-English Lexicon of the New Testament* (Grand Rapids: Zondervan, 1963), pp. 49, 427.

7. Thomas Lechford, *Plain Dealing: or, Newes from New-England;* In *Collections of the Massachusetts Historical Society*, 3d Series (Cambridge: E. W. Metcalf and Company, 1933) III:81, 398. The original manuscript is located in the Massachusetts Historical Society, 1154 Boylston St., Boston. Hereafter cited as Lechford, *Plain Dealing*.
Dale Miller, "Protestantism and Politics in Rhode Island," p. 39. Miller maintains that "religious liberty was...a cardinal ideal of the Bay." What he means, evidently, is that the only requirement of the law was "join the church and qualify for citizenship." To Clarke, however, this was little short of bowing to what he called "worldly worships," which will become apparent later in this work.

8. William P. Sheffield, "John Clarke, Physician, Philanthropist, Preacher and Patriot," p. 4. This was an oration delivered before the American Medical Association on June 25, 1889 and reprinted from *Journal of the American Medical Association*, August 24, 1889. Sheffield noted that the Massachusetts General Court enacted this into law on May 17, 1637.

9. Winthrop's *Journal* I:5. Author has been unable to find any documented evidence of Clarke's alliance with the Puritans.

10. Savage, *History of New England* I:Preface.

11. Winthrop's *Journal* I:277.

12. Ibid. 292.

13. Edward Winslow, *Hypocrisie Unmasked a True Relation of the Proceedings of the Governor and Company of the Massachusetts Against Samuel Gorton of Rhode Island* (Providence: Club for Colonial Reprints, 1916), p. 93, *et passim*. Reprinted from the Original Edition issued at London in 1646 with an introduction by Howard Millar Chapin. Gov. Winslow and ex-Gov. John Winthrop, Sr. represented Massachusetts at Whitehall in London against R. Is. on boundary disputes.

14. Clarke, *Ill Newes*, p. 24.

15. Winthrop's *Journal* I:298. Winthrop described Ezekiel as the second son of Richard Rogers of Weathersfield, England.

16. Clarke, *Ill Newes*, pp. 32, 33. It seems universally admitted that the Anabaptists as a distinct movement had their origin in Switzerland sometime between 1523 and 1525. Clarke repudiated the term Anabaptist because of its misapplication. The earliest group classified as Anabaptists were not Anabaptists at all. Led by the radical leader Thomas Muntzer, they revolted against the oppressive social and economic forces. The term Anabaptist in its more correct form applied to those who baptized a second time because they considered the first attempt as an invalid sign; the Anabaptists baptized only believers. Muntzer, in fact, was himself baptized as an infant, not as a believer. In the second century A.D., some called the Montanists Anabaptists because they baptized all those who came to them from other groups whom they considered improperly baptized.

17. Clarke, *Ill Newes,* pp. 23, 24; cf. Winthrop's *Journal* I:243–54.

18. Winthrop's *Journal* I:195.

19. Miller, "Protestantism and Politics in Rhode Island," pp. 21, 22.

20. Clarke, *Ill Newes*, pp. 23, 24.

21. Ibid.

22. Ibid.

23. Miller, "Protestantism and Politics in Rhode Island," p. 27. Editor Chapin believes that the party stopped at Boston on their way south from New Hampshire; after signing the compact, the party left Boston for Providence during the middle or latter part of March. This seems probable because the election of officers for their new government occurred on March 7, during which time the compact was framed.

24. Chapin, *History of Rhode Island* I:61. The original was left with William Arnold and became badly mutilated. Two copies were made and preserved, one by Thomas Olney and the other by William Harris. Both copies were accepted as correct and recorded on "7, 12 mo. 1658…"

25. Miller, "Protestantism and Politics in Rhode Island," p. 28. The names affixed to the document appeared in the following order: William Coddington; John Clarke; William Hutchinson, Jr.; John Coggeshall; William Aspinwall; Samuel Wilbore; John Porter; John Sanford; Edward Hutchinson, Jr., Esq.; Thomas Savage; William Dyre; William Freeborne; Phillip Shearman; John Walker; Richard Carder; William Baulston; Edward Hutchinson, Sen'r; Henry Bulle (his marke); Randall Holden. John Russell Bartlett, ed. *Records of the Colony of Rhode Island and Providence Plantations in New England, 1636–1663* (10 vols.; Providence: A. Crawford Greene and Brother, State Printers, 1856–1865) I:52. Hereafter cited as Bartlett, *Records of Rhode Island.*

26. Chapin, *History of Rhode Island* II:20.

27 Winthrop's *Journal* I:240

28. Ibid., p. 264.

29. Chapin, *History of Rhode Island* II:24.

Chapter IV
Pioneer Colonizer

The group which migrated from Boston to Rhode Island and signed the Portsmouth charter, along with the young English doctor John Clarke, included men of the highest social order. In characterizing their social standing, author Austen Kennedy DeBlois wrote, "In matters of social position and sound culture the best of Boston left Boston with Dr. John Clarke."[1]

The same day on which the Portsmouth contract was signed the colonists elected their first two officers of state. William Coddington was selected as the "judge" or presiding official, and William Aspinwall was appointed Secretary.[2] Obviously Coddington was the best qualified as well as the most popular choice of the Antinomians; he had served continuously in high office from his first arrival in Boston in 1630.[3] By virtue of his experience in jurisprudence, he seemed to them the logical choice.

As early as 1629, even before leaving England for America, Coddington was appointed assistant judge for the Massachusetts Bay Colony. This was probably due to his business relations of course. He was in the initial Puritan group to Boston, along with Winthrop and his Puritan stock company. Coddington was also probably more experienced in both political and business interests than any other man in the group.

Because of a religious emphasis and Old Testament influence on the compact, the charter may have presaged a kind of theocratic government. At least Chapin theorized such when he said that "apparently the signers of this compact planned to establish a theocratic state governed by their interpretation of the Holy Scriptures."[4] While this may have been true of Coddington and certain others, it hardly seems correct to say that of Dr. Clarke. On the contrary, Clarke, it seems, sought to help establish a government free of all religious restriction, one which in no way infringed upon the freedom of any religious conscience. This becomes evident from his remarks to the leaders of the established colonies upon his first arrival in Boston and by his subsequent activities throughout New England. Even though there were theocratic leanings among some of the Antinomians, Dr. Clarke, perhaps, hoped that the group would not set up such a government.

When the advance party first put in at Providence, the two champions of liberty, Roger Williams and Dr. Clarke, met for the first time.[5] They immediately became fast friends and associates, working together in a most harmonious manner, both socially and politically, throughout the remainder of Clarke's life.

A New Colony Established

After the Antinomian group stated its purpose of settlement, Williams suggested two places where they might settle: Sowames (presently called Barrington) and Aquidneck Island, both in the Narragansett Bay.[6] Unaware that either of these two places was under a patent to Plymouth, Williams suggested that the group inquire at Plymouth. In turn a committee of three, Clarke and two others, was appointed.[7] Together with Williams, the committee sailed for Plymouth.[8]

The Plymouth magistrates also met the group and "lovingly" but quickly informed them that "Sowames was the garden of their Patent." Clarke, in turn, assured them that their design was not to infringe upon another colony's rights nor was it their intention even to locate near a settled area. Rather their intention and desire, Clarke stated emphatically, was "to get cleer of all, and be of ourselves." When no jurisdiction over Aquidneck then was claimed, Clarke wrote that through the "occurrences of Providence" they obtained title to the island of Aquidneck and everyone was pleased.[9]

Through the helpful assistance of Williams, the migrate pioneers obtained a legal title for their new territory. On March 24, 1637/8[10] Williams drew up a document, which granted the pioneers a permanent home. The document was signed at Narragansett by two Sachem Indians, Caunounicus and Miantunnomue; it was witnessed by Roger Williams and Randall Holden.[11] According to Coddington, because the Sachem Wonnumetonomey on Aquidneck was unauthorized to make the transaction, the group proceeded from Aquidneck to Narragansett where the final agreement was completed.[12]

Because of the unusual purchase transaction for Aquidneck, later confusion and misunderstanding created dissension among some of the colonists. Some claimed the island was bought, whereas Williams objected to the term "bought." He argued the purchase was made possible only "by the love and favor" of Sir Henry Vane and himself; and, he maintained, "it was not price nor money that could have purchased Rhode Island."[13] However Williams suggested that the Sachems be given a token gift in exchange for the land; this unusual exchange of a "gratuity," according to the language of the bill of sale, was interpreted as a purchase price. In view of the documentary wording, the mercenary understanding seemed valid, as the essence of the record showed:

> That we Caunounicus and Miantunnomi the two chiefe Sachims of the Nanhiggansets…have sold unto Mr. Coddington and his friends united unto him, the great Island of Acquednecke lying from hence Eastward in this Bay…for the full payment of forty fathom of white beads, to be equally divided betweene us.[14]

Both Clarke and Coddington viewed the transaction as a purchase because, as Clarke explained: "Having bought them off to their full satisfaction, we have possessed the place ever since."[15] Many years later, the year following Clarke's death, Coddington signed a deposition on September 27,

1677, in which he used the term bought in describing the transaction.[16] Williams, of course, had cleared up the matter as early as 1638. In a letter to Winthrop in June of 1638, Williams wrote, "The truth is, not a penny was demanded for either, and what was paid was only gratuity, though I choose, for better assurance and form, to call it sale."[17]

According to Williams, when he drew up the deed, he penned it in Coddington's name, yet he included the names of others who accompanied Coddington. It seemed, of course, that it never entered Williams' mind to present the new land solely to Coddington to act as arbitrary governor. Nonetheless some years later when Coddington made a deposition of the facts relating to the purchase he included all of those involved in the plantation settlement. And Coddington confessed that Aquidneck was purchased following "an agreement of Eighteene persons to make purchase of some place to the southward for a plantation."[18]

Coddington was responsible to see that the gratuity which Williams advised was made. For that reason only, Williams claimed, he placed Coddington's name first on the list of purchasers. Quite sometime after the purchase, Gregory Dexter, the town clerk of Providence, printer, and Baptist minister wrote to Sir Henry Vane in England and expressed concern for the people of Rhode Island over the self-interest which Governor Coddington had shown with regard to the island purchase.[19] This seems to mark out the beginning of Judge (later Governor) Coddington's self-elevation in the colony; moreover it suggested further difficulty for Dr. Clarke and those of his Christian and predisposed freedom following.

With the legal ownership of Aquidneck secured, the hopeful colony settled down to begin a new way of life. The first settlement on the island was called Pocasset; after the founding of Newport, it was renamed Portsmouth.[20] From the records it appears that during the first ten years of settlement, Dr. Clarke was more actively engaged in the two major professions of medicine and the ministry than he was in politics. As the only recognized physician and minister among the colonists, it would seem he was very busy. Perhaps his talents were in greater demand in these two areas. Still Dr. Clarke contributed his share in aiding the infant colony. Even though he was very involved, whenever necessary, he responded to every request for help. With clear abandon, he demonstrated his eagerness to assist in whatever way he was needed.

THE FIRST CHURCH BUILDING IN PORTSMOUTH

The first General Meeting of the Portsmouth government convened on May 13, 1638, and Clarke was one of thirteen men present. Matters of general interest to the colonists were dealt with and expedited efficiently. The apportionment of land, a mutual defense of the territory, and provision for a "Meeting House" were ordered.[21] At this point, Chapin states emphatically that the church in Portsmouth was a state-church. In the absence of any evidence, however, to substantiate such a claim, this appears to be an unwarranted supposition. After all it seems clear that the entire group was too independent to set up any type of religious theocracy. Of course there were among them strong divisive and self-centered opinions, as it proved in later separations.

Indeed Clarke's subsequent disclaimers against a state church of any kind (and without even a hint of change in religious ideas) seem to suggest that Clarke did not leave Boston in order to establish the same kind of church from which he sought refuge. His later condemnation of such a congregation and his remarkable compatibility with his philosophy of civil and religious freedom tend to refute Chapin's claim. On the other hand, however, since the building project was a community effort, it would appear that the building structure was intended for public use. Naturally, since Clarke was the only preacher among them, it might be taken for granted that he made use of it, regardless of his exclusive denominational ties at that time or even the religious affiliations of the others. At the next meeting, held on May 20, 1638, Clarke was granted an apportionment of six acres of land, an amount equal to the others.[22]

THE EMERGENCE OF AN AUTOCRACY

True to the anticipation of some, matters at Portsmouth soon became confused and disorderly. Tension mounted as dissatisfaction arose over the manner in which Coddington ruled the colony. He remained the sole executive officer, of course, until the first election, which was held on January 2, 1639. At this election, Coddington acceded to the Hutchinson faction and acquiesced in permitting the creation of a board of three elders. This board was designed to assist the magistrate in town affairs. According to Chapin, this was an ingenious move by Coddington, aimed at retaining his political influence in Portsmouth by strengthening his position. As it happened, of course, those appointed were his own political followers.[23]

The absence of Clarke's participation in ruling affairs at this point seems obvious—perhaps too obvious—in view of his previous initiative and active involvement in the colony's interest. It hardly seems likely that he was being willfully neglected, especially since his name appeared second to Coddington's in the original compact. It probably indicates that he was not pleased with the autocratic direction of Coddington, so he was busily engaged in what he deemed were more important duties of the moment, still hoping for a better turn of events.

Individualism, apparently, was too marked among the new settlers. Perhaps the sudden taste of uninhibited freedom created unrest, which resulted in dissension within the initial group that perilously approached anarchy. In addition the recent arrival of new immigrants—who manifested religious beliefs antagonistic toward the Coddington group—enhanced the Hutchinson faction and evidently gave force to an overt expression of dissatisfaction. As Chapin maintained, however, Coddington had asserted a strong autocratic rule from the outset. Then the arrival of others who were perhaps more independent-minded merely provided the impetus for an uprising, an upheaval which from the outset presaged a serious separation within the Antinomian group at Portsmouth.[24]

Governor Winthrop heard of the unrest at Portsmouth and the impending breakup of the newly established colony. He promptly made note of it. On May 11, 1639, shortly after the colony divided, he recorded in his *Journal* the following notation:

> At Aquiday the people grew very tumultuous, and put out Mr. Coddington and the other three magistrates, and chose Mr. William Hutchinson only, a man of a very mild temper and weak parts, and wholly guided by his wife, who had been the beginner of all the former troubles in the country, and still continued to breed disturbance.[25]

The only public service at Portsmouth which Clarke was appointed to perform was that of a survey committee. The records state that "Mr. Clarke with Mr. Jefferies & John Porter & Richard Burden shall survey all the Lands near abouts."[26] It seems that this task was never completed because on April 28, 1639, during an absence of Coddington, the Hutchinson faction called a town meeting and, according to Chapin, executed a *coup d'etat* against the government.[27]

Further Division and Separation

Following the election of a new judge, Coddington, William Dyre, and seven of the others among the Antinomian group withdrew. Obviously Coddington refused to submit to the unexpected public shift of opinion because he and his closest associates hastily left Portsmouth. Dr. Clarke was among the nine original settlers who left and migrated to the southwest tip of Aquidneck; there they founded the town of Newport on May 1, 1639 (according to the notes of Nicholas Easton's son Peter—as recorded by Chapin).[28]

Although Dr. Clarke may have been disappointed in Coddington's autocratic leadership, nonetheless he probably preferred him over the unstable Antinomians, especially for the time being. It would seem that now Dr. Clarke approached a time in which he could no longer identify with the Antinomians, even though he probably harbored uncomfortable feelings about Coddington. As it happened, it was simply a matter of time before Dr. Clarke would reveal his religious opposition to Judge Coddington and some of his followers, which becomes apparent below.

CHAPTER IV ENDNOTES

1. Austen Kennedy deBlois, *Fighters for Freedom, Heroes of the Baptist Challenge* (Philadelphia: Judson Press, 1929), p. 165.

2. Chapin, *History of Rhode Island*, II:21.

3. *Winthrop's Journal*, I:270.

4. Chapin, *History of Rhode Island*, II:20.

5. It is interesting to note that both Williams and Clarke proclaimed individual human rights and liberty several years before the celebrated John Locke's philosophy appeared. Since they were contemporaries and probably acquainted, it would seem that their convictions may have had some impact on Locke. A further study here could prove enlightening.

6. Clarke, *Ill Newes*, p. 24.

7. Ibid. Chapin suggests that the two others were Coddington and Holden, but he conjectures that probably William Hutchinson; John Sanford, Sr.; John Porter; Richard Carder; and William Dyre accompanied the committee and may have been an integral part of it.

8. Chapin, *History of Rhode Island*, II:24.

9. Clarke, *Ill Newes*, pp. 24–5.

10. Chapin, *History of Rhode Island*, II:22. The dating system used by those early settlers of Rhode Island was very confusing. Their new year began on March 1. In the Old Style—used in England and parts of New England—the new year began on March 25. Thus this date, Mar. 24, 1637, was the last day of 1637. In the New Style (the modern one), the new year begins on January 1.

11. Ibid., I:51.

12. Chapin, *History of Rhode Island*, II.

13. Bartlett, *Letters of Roger Williams*, VI:305–306.

14. Chapin, *History of Rhode Island*, II:26–7.

15. Clarke, *Ill Newes*, p. 25.

16. Chapin, *History of Rhode Island*, II:26.

17. Bartlett, *Letters of Roger Williams*, VI:104, 306.

18. Chapin, *History of Rhode Island*, II:29. The discrepancy between the number eighteen purchasers and Chapin's nineteen signers is explained in Isaac Backus, *History of the Baptists*, I:78. Editor Weston explains that since Holden acted as a witness to the Aquidneck deed, it seemed that he was not interested in the purchase. Because of this, he was not included as one of the purchasers but only acted as a witness to the agreement.

19. Bartlett, *Letters of Roger Williams*, VI:266–68. The letter was prepared by Williams; evidently, he made the censure.

20. Chapin, *History of Rhode Island*, II:219.

21. Ibid., II:35–6.

22. Bartlett, *Records of Rhode Island*, I:55.

23. Chapin, *History of Rhode Island*, II:48.

24. Ibid.

25. Winthrop's *Journal*, I:299.

26. Chapin, *History of Rhode Island*, II:49–50.

27. Ibid., pp. 56–9.

28. Ibid., pp 57, 69.

Chapter V
Emerging Democracy

The small band of pioneers, which split off from the main Antinomian group at Portsmouth and migrated to the southern tip of Rhode Island, had chosen for themselves a land of serenic beauty and soon manifested their optimistic outlook for the future. Early in the sixteenth century an Italian-born French corsair, Giovanni da Verrazzano, explored the harbor of Newport, Rhode Island. Sailing under the flag of Francois I of France, Verrazzano dropped anchor in the harbor on April 21, 1524. He compared the size of present Rhode Island to that of "the Island of the Rodes." He described its geographical layout as "full of hills covered with trees." The island he found well populated—obviously, with American Indians—as he said, "We sawe fires all along the coasts."[1]

From 1639 to 1649, the town of Newport progressed rapidly. For a while the new colony remained under the type of leadership which was set up at Portsmouth. Coddington, as chief magistrate, continued his control over the town.[2] His power was further enhanced when the magistrate was given a double vote, an addition made before the Coddington faction withdrew from Portsmouth.[3]

Among his other talents, Dr. Clarke seemed to possess a patient and understanding spirit. Apparently in view of his busy activities he never involved himself in political affairs. His first public service of any note was an appointment to a survey committee in June of 1639, whose assignment was to survey and "lay out all the Lands for the Towns accommodations."[4] Later in the year, Clarke and William Brenton (one of three Elders selected to assist Judge Coddington) were appointed to a trade investigation committee. The committee was instructed to investigate certain differences that arose over trade with the Indians.[5]

On December 25, Clarke was appointed to a committee of two, whose assignment was to write a diplomatic letter to Sir Henry Vane in England, pursuant to obtaining a "Patent for the island."[6] This action, perhaps, revealed Dr. Clarke's true concern about a theocracy and Judge Coddington's autocratic rule; at any rate, it marked the real beginning of Clarke's active involvement in public service of the infant colony. Clarke and others had been patient with the ruling group, but the growing threat of autocracy became alarming to them.

Matters of a dominating autocratic government under Judge Coddington became a grave concern for Dr. Clarke and perhaps for certain others among the Newport settlers. Soon it became evident to them that vital changes in political structure were necessary in order to secure a free society. Meanwhile autocratic rule prevailed in Newport. On March 12, 1640, the towns of Newport and Portsmouth united under a single government. Then Coddington was elected governor of the entire island.[7]

THE FIRST COLONIAL DEMOCRACY

There remained a growing concern of Coddington's rule among the inhabitants at Newport. By 1641, a bold and progressive step was taken by the Rhode Islanders. At their General Court of election, held at Portsmouth from March 15–19, 1641, they officially affirmed and recorded their new rule as a "Democracie."[8] The nature of this political structure at this point, of course, was that of a limited democracy. The body of electors was relatively small, consisting only of property owners; yet their disposition on both civil and religious freedoms was clearly stated. The ruling body reaffirmed its liberal position on such freedoms, and the record—as cited by Rhode Island Secretary of State John Russell Bartlett—appeared as follows:

> It is ordered and unanimously agreed upon, that the government which this Bodie Politick doth attend unto in this Island, and the Jurisdiction thereof, in favour of our Prince is a DEMOCRACIE, or Popular Government; that is to say, It is in the Powre of the Body of Freemen orderly assembled, or the major part of them, to make or constitute Just Lawes…It was further ordered, by the authority of this present Courte, it be not directly repugnant to ye Government or Lawes stablished.[9]

Independent interests now became subordinated to community interests—but with projected measures—in order to offset any further autocratic or theocratic rule. Optimistic about this realization, the colony sought to establish safeguards in their governmental structure by creating a General Council made up of "Freemen" or property-owning citizens. By this new innovation, both social and religious freedom would be secured, and equal justice would be guaranteed to all citizens. To be sure, this type of government seemed to have been Dr. Clarke's personal goal from the beginning.

Again Clarke was assigned to a committee on correspondence to write Henry Vane about a patent.[10] The Newport inhabitants now sought a closer union with Providence, and Clarke was assigned to write Vane spearheading such proposed union.

At the Quarter Session meeting in Portsmouth, Clarke was appointed to a three-man committee on arbitration. This committee was formed to arbitrate a legal suit between Captain Robert Harding and William Withington.[11] Again, on October 8, 1646, Clarke was appointed to a similar committee, except this time it was an eight-man arbitration committee for the Quarter Session Court, which had convened at Newport two days earlier, on October 6, 1646.[12]

Between the years 1644 and 1647, several attempts were made to unify the four towns of the island under one centralized government. On March 13, 1644, the General Court held at Newport changed the island name Aquidneck to that of Rhode Island.[13] At that time, Roger Williams was in England in an effort to secure a charter for Providence and adjacent areas; in turn he was granted a "Parliamentary commission" on March 14, 1644, which came under the heading of "Providence Plantations." Williams then returned to Boston on September 17 of the same year.[14]

Considerable dissension arose over the ratification of the patent, but by May 21, 1647, all four towns, Portsmouth, Newport, Providence, and Warwick had acquiesced to the proposed unification. The island government then came under a more centralized colonial rule and henceforth became known as the Province of Providence Plantations. Despite these political alterations, Governor Coddington continued his unrelinquishing effort to maintain his political control.[15]

By 1647, Dr. Clarke's prolific talents were unquestionably felt in all of Rhode Island. Baptist historian Albert Henry Newman, in fact, argued that Clarke was the principal author of the Code of Laws, which the united colony adopted in 1647.[16]

In the year 1648, eleven years after the young doctor offered his significant motion to resettle, Clarke accepted an active role in the politics of Rhode Island. Evidently by this time the colonists recognized a valuable asset in Dr. Clarke. Even Roger Williams alluded to his prominence. On May 16, Clarke was elected Commissioner for the town of Newport. At the same election, he was appointed to a four-man Accusation committee for the General Court of Trials. The next year Clarke was elected General Treasurer and General Assistant for Newport; he was reelected to both offices in 1650.[17]

Now the talented English-American added law and politics to his already crowded professions of medicine and religious ministry. As time proved, Dr. Clarke became a true servant to the people; indeed he would serve in several history-making roles. Soon his multiple talents and dedication to the growing colony would become well known throughout both New England at large and the Old England commonwealth as well.

As a servant of the people, Dr. Clarke would steer the colony toward a government of unprecedented civil and religious liberty—convinced that any other move would be in the direction of a self-centered autocratic theocracy. Not all of Clarke's associates, of course, concurred with such a ruling philosophy; in fact at that stage of development two opposite philosophies of government loomed large. At one extreme was the new democratic experiment with its attending threat of anarchy and all of its evils of disorder, violence, and ultimate chaos. On the other hand stood the growing menace of autocratic rule and its restrictions on all forms of liberty. Clarke was aware of these opposing threats; after all all of the colonists had been living under this latter type of government and had experienced first hand its kindred evils of civil and religious restrictions. As it happened, Clarke would choose to steer a course between the treacherous rapids of anarchy and the imposing threat of stifled civil and religious freedoms. Given the choice, the people then opted to follow Dr. Clarke.

For many years Dr. Clarke was one of the most effective leaders of Rhode Island. In addition to his busy duties of state, he always found time to help those who needed him, and he remained steadily engaged in the active ministry of the Baptist faith. No evidence has appeared to indicate that Clarke ever wavered in either of his religious convictions or loyal service to Rhode Island, his new colonial home.

CHAPTER V ENDNOTES

1. Chapin, *History of Rhode Island*, II:1. According to Chapin, the earliest use of the name Rhode Island appeared in a letter by Roger Williams who made the following passing remark in 1637: "The provisions and munitions first arrive at Aquetnetick, called by us Rode-Island"; ibid., p. 15.

2. Ibid., I:223.

3. Ibid., II:57–8, 71.

4. Bartlett, *Records of Rhode Island*, I:88–9, 94.

5. Ibid.

6. Ibid., 99.

7. Ibid., 100.

8. Ibid., 112–13.

9. Ibid.

10. Ibid., 125. Chapin writes, because of the records which have survived, it is uncertain whether action was taken by these committees; he conjectures, however, subsequent events indicate there was.

11. Chapin, *History of Rhode Island*, II:143–44. The Writ was transcribed on September 8, 1643, by Harding and Withington; ibid., p. 145.

12. Ibid., 156.

13. Bartlett, *Records of Rhode Island*, I:127.

14. Chapin, *History of Rhode Island*, I:212, 214, 219.

15. Bartlett, *Records of Rhode Island*, I:147, 150. Chapin attributes this difficulty to the political ambitions of Coddington. Chapin, *History of Rhode Island*, I:222–23.

16. Albert Henry Newman, *A History of the Baptist Churches in the United States* (New York: Christian Literature, 1894), p. 100.

17. Bartlett, *Records of Rhode Island*, I:209, 208, 212–13, 216–17, 220–21; *Letters of Roger William's*, VI:150, 183–84.

Chapter VI
Religious Innovator

Among those who sought asylum from the established religions of the Bay, Dr. Clarke proved to be the most stable-minded and firmly entrenched in his convictions. As an unclassified preacher among the vacillating group, Clarke found himself in strange company. Since no record of his conversion has been discovered, as yet it appears uncertain when Clarke became a Baptist. Even though unwitting writers have written that Clarke was a Puritan when he arrived in the New World, no contemporary of his has documented the claim.

The assumption that Clarke came to America as a Baptist is not unusual because Baptists kept few records at that early date. Moreover Baptists did not identify themselves by that name nor did they accept the opprobrium of Anabaptist because, to them, it falsely identified their beliefs and practices. Neither, by and large, did Baptists make their records public for some time after this period. For the above reasons, and the lack of specifics at the time of Clarke's arrival in Boston, they do not in themselves tell us Dr. Clarke underwent a religious change some time after his arrival in New England.

Even the name Baptist was not generally accepted by Baptists at large until well into the eighteenth century. Usually in their correspondences the salutary addresses followed a style similar to the following: "The Church at Boston Baptized upon profession of faith...on ye 14th and 15th April, 1668."[1] Quite often the Baptists labeled their churches as a "church of Christ." As late as 1727, in fact, in a letter dated September 7, 1727, a Baptist church letter of correspondence read as follows: "From a church of Christ in Swanzey to a church of Christ at Newport."[2]

Although one of the first items of business by the settlers of Portsmouth was the provision for a Meeting House, it has not been determined whether the building was ever erected. Be that as it may, the lack of a special building set aside as a meeting place, of course, would not have prevented religious services for Baptists or even the organization of a church.

In fact the church that Dr. Clarke founded and pastored, called "The United Baptist Church John Clarke Memorial," stated, "The (initial founding) group came to the Island of Aquidneck in March, 1638, and settled on the north end of the island in the general area of the present Sakonnet River Bridge. There in a home a church was organized." It was located at the place "known locally as Green End, inland from Easton's Beach. There they built the first meeting house."[3] While this claim is only tradition, the church's Historical Tracts continue to say that strong probability exists that "in an old house in

Southeastern Massachusetts or Eastern Connecticut these records may be lost in dust and mold."[4] A special church bulletin of 1965, then, stated that Clarke founded a church at Portsmouth and moved the congregation to Newport in 1639.

Rhode Island historian and pastor John Callender claimed that Clarke "carried on a publick Worship (as Mr. Brewster did at Plymouth) at the first coming, till they procured Mr. Lenthal of Weymouth."[5] The precise meaning of Callender's statement is uncertain; nonetheless what is certain is that Robert Lenthal was a Puritan minister when he arrived in New England. But there is not a record known to the author that gives Lenthal as pastor or even assistant pastor of the church in Newport.

The first public notice of a church in Rhode Island appears in Winthrop's writings. His reference to the religious disposition of the colonists at Aquidneck was penned in May 1639, which was cited in the previous chapter. However some disagreement exists with regard to the group that Winthrop alluded. Of course the words of the preceding paragraph, "At Aquiday the people grew very tumultuous, and put out Mr. Coddington and the other three magistrates,"[6] would indicate that Winthrop meant those among the Anne Hutchinson faction at Portsmouth. This seems evident by the antecedent "they" who overthrew Coddington and his followers. Clarke of course was among those who left Portsmouth with Coddington.

Sometime later, in fact, both elements from Portsmouth and Newport refused to honor church messengers sent from the Bay churches. Winthrop indeed recorded that the church would not accept letters from their Puritan congregations. On March 24, 1640, he wrote,

> when they came, they found that those of them, who dwell at Newport, had joined themselves to a church there newly constituted, and thereupon they refused to hear them as messengers of our church, or to receive the church's letters.[7]

Elder Robert Lenthal accompanied the committee; they first stopped at Portsmouth and the next month traveled to Newport.[8] Contemporary testimony stated that a church was extant the same year that Newport was settled. Editor Chapin recorded that Governor Coddington wrote on December 9, 1639, "I am removed 12 myles further up in the Iland. Ther they have gathered a Church & doe intend to chuse officers shortely."[9]

Since only a small number removed to Newport, new church officers probably were necessary. This would explain Coddington's statement pursuant to the election of officers. Several reasons could be given to account for this further selection of leaders, all of which conform even to present-day practice of Baptist polity. Indeed most churches hold annual election of officers.

It appears beyond doubt, then, that some kind of church existed in Rhode Island from its earliest settlement and that Dr. Clarke was the organizer and first pastor. Available evidence as to the nature of the church is not entirely lacking either. The unquestioned refusal of the Newport group to cooperate with either the Separatist churches of Plymouth colony or Puritans of the Massachusetts Bay area denote that from the outset the church was of a more rigid separatist order, like the Baptists.

Likewise minister Robert Lenthal probably became a Baptist very early. He migrated to Boston from Surrey, England, sometime during 1637. He was twenty-one years old and a clergyman when he arrived in Boston.[10] Winthrop wrote that the people of Weymouth invited Lenthal to be their minister shortly after he arrived in Boston. Winthrop further said that Lenthal had a good reputation in England, but after he arrived in Boston he "drank in some of Mrs. Hutchinson's opinions, as of justification before faith, etc., and opposed the gathering of our churches in such a way—that only baptism was the door of entrance into the church." Lenthal further attempted, Winthrop argued, "to get such a church on foot as all baptized ones might communicate in without any further trial of them, etc."[11]

Assuming Lenthal came to Boston as a Puritan minister, then it become evident that Anabaptist teachings were propagated by 1638, strong enough to impact the young minister. Unless, of course, Lenthal underwent a change in religious convictions prior to leaving his homeland for America and his Puritan friends never learned of it. On the other hand, if he did undergo such a change after arriving in the New World, it was most likely between his arrival and 1639, because Winthrop wrote of his preaching on January 30, 1639, and it was shortly after the date of the letter that he was admitted a Freeman of Massachusetts. By May 20, 1639, of course, he was an inhabitant of Newport. Since Lenthal accompanied the Puritan church committee from Massachusetts back to Newport in 1640, it seems at times that he traveled back to Massachusetts.[12] He was not admitted a Freeman of Newport, however, until August 6, 1640.[13]

Lenthal's stay in America was short, yet he rendered valuable service to the community during his stay in Rhode Island. He has been described as a helper of Newport in general and of Clarke in particular. He was the first public school teacher in America, according to the state records.[14] Clarke and Lenthal were social and religious partners from Lenthal's first arrival in Newport, but no light has been shed on whether either one baptized the other.

Another minister, Hanserd Knollys, who became a non-conformist in England and came to New England for awhile, was later identified with Clarke and Lenthal among the Particular Baptists of London. Knollys was from Lincoln County, England. For a time, he was a Presbyterian, "having walked with them." He was ordained a deacon on September 19, 1629, and a presbyter the next day. But he came to differ with them in their church way; they required only faith, repentance, and baptism, and they did not enter into any form of covenant; as Knollys expressed it, "without urging or making any particular covenant with members upon admittance." Knollys came to hold that one is received a member by consent of a particular church.

According to this, of course, one could be baptized yet be rejected as a member.[15]

Knollys became troubled about his Presbyterian ordination, but in 1631 he felt a call to preach. After preaching for some three or four years—all the while being hounded by authorities—Knollys moved to London, where in 1636, he was imprisoned. A sympathetic jailer, however, helped him to escape, and Knollys fled to London and booked passage to America.[16]

William Buell Sprague believed that Knollys became a Baptist before he boarded a ship for New England. He based his notion on a letter dated April 28, 1859, in which a Reverend Dr. Belcher maintained that Knollys was baptized while awaiting passage to America.[17] Editor Weston noted that "in 1636 [Knollys], publicly joined the Dissenters" of London and fled to America. This was possible as Knollys, his wife, and their small child had to wait two years for passage. The child died enroute, and the Knollys arrived at Boston in 1638, penniless, forcing Knollys to earn his living with a garden hoe.[18]

Shortly after the family arrived in New England, Knollys was arrested and charged with Antinomiansim. When he was examined and found holding "familistical" opinions he was denied residence in Massachusetts. A friend in turn took him to his plantation at Dover (Piscataqua) where Knolllys preached and "gathered some of the best minded into a church body, and became their pastor" until 1641, at which time he returned to England because of his aging father.[19]

While on his friend's plantation, Knollys founded the church shortly after September 1638, the first church in Dover and perhaps in the New Hampshire Colony. In 1640, difficulty arose between Thomas Larkham and the church; Larkham took certain of the members and formed another body. The dispute was over Larkham's believe in baptizing children and the reception of church members.[20]

Following Knollys' return to England, that same year the church of Dover moved to Long Island, New York. When the island fell to the British in 1664, the congregation settled on the East side of the Raritan River in New Jersey, a colony still under the Dutch. There the church settled a town which they named Dover (Piscataway), New Jersey. From 1689 to 1739, John Drake—a descendent of Sir Francis Drake, the famous explorer—pastored the church. All the while, the church was called a Baptist church.

Upon his return to London, Knollys first taught school. The next year, 1642, he organized a church in London, evidently, the "Bow [Lane] Church," later known as the Coleman Street Baptist Church. A ministerial associate, William Kiffin, wrote that Knollys was with a church in London for nearly fifty years. Time and again, however, Knollys was arrested for preaching without a license; during the years 1643 to 1645, when pressed to reveal his authority to preach, Knollys informed the investigating committee he was "ordained since in a church of God, according to the order of the gospel of Christ."[21]

In 1645, Knollys baptized Henry Jessey, who became the third pastor of the Jacob/Lathorp/Jessey Independent congregation, and the same or following year Knollys published an answer to the charge of a "new baptism."[22] As pastor of the Coleman Street Baptist Church in 1654, Knollys was in corresponding fellowship with the ancient Lollard-Anabaptist congregation at Warrington called Hill Cliffe.[23] English Baptist author Alfred Clair Underwood claimed that Knollys became involved in the Fifth Monarchy Movement from 1657 onward. Even though Knollys was arrested and charged with complicity in 1660, along with "other godly and peaceable persons," he denied any connections with Venner and Fifth monarchy.[24]

Evidently during those troubled times for the British, Knollys was seriously threatened in his ministry. It was noted that "a man with a crossbow had lately shot bullets at the noted leader of the Baptists, Hanserd Knollys"; however the offender was caught.[25]

Knollys was very talented. Not only was he a teacher of grammar, he also compiled Latin, Greek, and Hebrew grammars.[26] Although Knollys denied the special Charismata gifts of the early Christian ministry, he did pray for the sick, including himself.[27]

Meanwhile what about Dr. Clarke and the church at Newport? Again attorney Lechford spoke of those at Newport, as follows: "At the Island called Aquedney, are about two hundred families. There was a Church, where one master Clark was Pastor; There is Mr. Lenthall a minister out of office and imployment, and lives poorly. Mr. Doughty also is come to this Island. The place where the church is, is called New porte."[28] While Lechford said nothing about Clarke's Anabaptist persuasion, neither did he mention Lenthal's, so we only have Winthrop's remarks. Lechford did, however, say that those of Providence were mostly Anabaptists and that there was no church at Portsmouth.[29]

QUAKERISM IN NEW ENGLAND

The diverse doctrines, previously manifested by those at Portsmouth and certain ones of those who migrated to Newport, led to schism in the Newport church. Winthrop was quick to grasp the import of this. Sometime after April 13, 1641, in fact, Winthrop wrote,

> There joined with Nicholas Easton Mr. Coddington, Mr. Coggeshall, and some others, but their minister, Mr. Clarke, and Mr. Lenthall, and Mr. Harding, and some others dissented and publicly opposed, whereby it grew to such heat of contention that it made a schism among them.[30]

The dissension became so pronounced that Coddington, Coggeshall, Easton, and a few others withdrew; most others, in time, became Quakers.

The doctrinal concerns stemmed from the "belief that men must look to the revelation of an inner light which was to be followed, rather than the Scriptural word," according to editor Richard M. Bayles.[31] Elders Clarke, Lenthal, and certain others of the church opposed this notion and claimed that both Scripture and the Holy Spirit are two guides for Christians, not simply an "inner light." Of course this incident in 1641 marked the first shakings of Quakerism in Rhode Island; soon Quakerism flourished in the colony.

While the dissenters may have been members of the congregation in "full communion," it seems improbable. Since this was the only church gathering in the vicinity, the dissenters may only have attended services there. Such a notion was suggested by Coddington's remark, "they" plan to choose officers. Had Coddington been a member in good standing, it seems unlikely that he would have excused himself from such an important responsibility.

ANARCHY TENDENCIES

Meanwhile Winthrop spoke of further religious developments among those at Portsmouth, which bordered on anarchy:

> Mrs. Hutchinson and those of Aquiday island broached new heresies every year. Divers of them turned professed Anabaptists, and would not wear any arms, and denied all magistracy among Christians, and maintained that there were no churches since those founded by the apostles and evangelists, nor could any be, nor any pastors ordained, no seals administered but by such, and that the church was to want these all the time she continued in the wilderness, as yet she was.[32]

Indeed such were the sentiments of Anne Hutchinson and her group, yet it was not true to the facts concerning Clarke and his company. Clarke, in fact, clearly denied most of these opinions and expressed his opposition against both the new Anabaptists at Portsmouth and the Puritan order. Nevertheless Clarke claimed Governor John Endicott of Massachusetts called him an Anabaptist and charged him with anarchy in his rebellion against the Massachusetts authority.[33]

To those of course who really knew Clarke, such notions were unwarranted allegations. However, to the Puritan Elders, Clarke was guilty by association. In turn he became an accessory to all the diverse theological opinions which were spread throughout the territory. But the records unmistakably revealed that Clarke was strongly inclined toward a well-ordered civil government. Although the Portsmouth group refused to bear arms, the Newport inhabitants subscribed to a ready defense force. It was a misdemeanor, in fact, to frequent public places without a weapon. This law was among the earliest codes of the Newport government.[34]

A MOST STRICT NON-CONFORMITY

Relative to spiritual matters, Clarke denied that the church was then in the wilderness. He did concur, however, with Roger Williams and the Portsmouth Antinomians that the Puritan churches of the Bay were not proper churches because they were not constituted according to the New Testament pattern. Indeed it was for his flagrant denunciation of the Puritan Congregational order that Williams, his wife, Anne Hutchinson, and certain others were excluded from the Congregational Church at Salem, Massachusetts. Pastor Hugh Peters wrote to the church of Dorchester in order to acquaint the church with the disposition of those expelled, according to a letter by pastor Peters and recorded by chronicler Edwards. The reason for their censure Peters claimed, was because they "wholly refused to hear the church [denying it and all the churches in the Bay to be true churches]."[35]

As it happened, Clarke denounced most of the basic religious teachings both of the Hutchinson faction and the Puritan system, and it seems he had both of these in mind when he wrote the following apology:

> God forbid that thou shouldst be as one that wilt turn aside by the flocks of his companions, and shouldst be found remaining either on the left side in a visible way of worship in deed, but such as was neither appointed by Christ, nor yet practiced by them who first trusted in him,[36] or on the right in no visible way of worship, or order at all, either pretending that the outward court is given to the Gentiles, and the holy City is by them to be troden under foot; that the Church of Christ is now in the wilderness, and the time of its recovery is not yet.[37]

In this brief exhortation Clarke demonstrated his theological disagreement with all the separatist religious persuasions in the Bay area: Pilgrims, Puritans, Antinomians, Quakers, and even the Seeker Roger Williams.

ORIGIN OF FIRST BAPTIST CHURCH OF NEWPORT

The year 1644 stands as the date most commonly assigned for the church at Newport becoming a Baptist church. John Comer was the fifth pastor of the church; in his diary, he cites the record of Samuel Hubbard who states the church was "constituted about 1644." Hubbard was baptized and received into the church in 1648, and he names fifteen members of the church that year in his notes, the document that Comer discovered and used in his diary.[38] From this it would appear that the church as Baptist was founded before 1648, and Hubbard only heard it was begun about 1644. John Callender followed Comer as pastor in 1731, and he noted, "It is said, that in 1644, Mr. John Clark, and some others, formed a church, on the Scheme and Principles of the Baptists." It appears quite certain that in 1648, there were "fifteen Members in full Communion."[39]

REGULAR AND NON-REGULAR MEMBERS

The phrase full communion may be the solution to the question concerning both the nature and origin of the church at Newport. As late as 1680, both Baptists and Quakers were numerous; both enjoyed unprecedented liberties around Newport, yet the churches numbered very few members in regular order. Still many of those who were looked upon as members—by others at least—were not regularly baptized, by Baptist standards. Thus they were not considered in full communion.

Chronicler Edwards recorded that in 1771, about 250 families were considered a part of the church [at Providence], yet only 118 persons were "baptized and in communion."[40] Edwards cited the same twelve members in the Newport church for the year 1644 that pastor Callender listed: "Rev. John Clark and wife; Mark Lukar; John Peckham; John Thorndon; William Weeden and Samuel Weeden."[41]

The present congregation holds to 1638 as the date for the origin of the church as Baptist. They maintain that "since people did not cross back and forth over denominational lines in that early date, the people in Boston must have embraced Baptist views."[42]

An early member and Baptist minister of the church, Elder Mark Lucar (Lukar), came from England and settled at Newport in 1644. A hatmaker by trade, Lucar was arrested for nonconformity in London and confined in Old Bailey jail from 1632 to 1634. As a member of the first Particular Baptist Church of London from its earliest inception, he was associated with minister Richard Blount. Author George A. Lofton contended that Lucar brought immersion to the Newport congregation.[43] To be sure, Lucar was well acquainted with baptism by immersion. His proposed relation to Cyril Lucar, Patriarch of the Greek Orthodox Church of Alexandria, Egypt, in 1602, evidences this because the Greek branch of Christianity never abandoned this mode.[44]

Lucar became a Baptist in London before he migrated to Rhode Island, and English Baptist author William Thomas Whitley wrote he was baptized about 1642. Along with others, as shown below, Lucar became a member of a Baptist church that was organized in London in 1644, evidently just prior to Lucar's embarking for America. "In 1641/2, Thomas Kilcop, Lucar and Blunt were baptized; with Webb they headed a church emerging in 1644. Benjamin Cox joined by 1646, Edward Harrison by 1651, Samuel Tull by 1657."[45]

Based on the known primary evidence, the church at Newport, until 1644, could have undergone, perhaps, at least two stages of development. In the beginning it was probably constituted as a loosely gathered group of believers on the basis of "mixed communion," holding to the freedom of conscience and a separation of church and state.[46] The early rejection of any religious fellowship by Clarke and his following with the Puritans may have been because of the Puritan religious intolerance and church order. In the proposed change in organization in 1641, then, membership requirement became more strict, requiring baptism by immersion. Since immersion was practiced some in New England before this time, such a suggestion presents a concern for some modern Baptist authors (cf. Asher, "The Life and Letters of John Clarke").

At no time did Coddington ever claim that he was a member of the Church at Newport in regular standing. Until the seventeenth century, Baptists did not make public their religious activities. For centuries, in their practice of church/state separation, they considered their churches as separate from society, when any threat of encroachments on church polity and communion arose.[47] The Baptists have always considered church problems to be a concern of each local church; such was the case when Governor Coddington and others adopted Quakerism at its inception in Newport. Such a concern created a need for action by the church.

Along with Lenthal's help in 1641, the church may have surged ahead with a more clearly defined church polity. As yet, of course, no delineated doctrinal rules may have been apparent other than those already learned from experience, that is, those needed to maintain a harmonious church fellowship. By 1644, when Lucar joined the group, he could have brought the strict Baptist order from the British Baptists, which constituted the church along more modern lines. Yet Lucar may have treated the church as a mission church, and the church without any visible changes in practice or doctrine voted to cooperate with the Particular Baptists of London. Soon after this, in fact, such a church posture was publicly revealed without any indication of reorganization.[48]

All that can be said because of known documents already has been noted. Perhaps a former pastor of the Newport church said it best. He recorded that "Clarke founded a church in Portsmouth in 1638 which included a number of Baptists in its congregation, but did not become in name a Baptist church until a later date."[49] Pastor Wilbur Cheesman Nelson further claimed that good reasons exist to believe that Clarke was a Baptist before he left England and that he came to this country as "a Baptist refugee."[50]

Clarke's unwavering posture at this point stamped him among his contemporaries as perhaps the most stable-minded man socially and religiously in the political development of Rhode Island. Religiously virtually every opposing faction with which Clarke identified himself in the beginning splintered off into either the Hutchinson group, which ended in religious anarchy, or into Quakerism, with Governor Coddington and his associates.

CHAPTER VI ENDNOTES

1. Clarke Papers, Newport Historical Society.

2. Clarke Papers; In Collection of Backus Papers, Rhode Island Historical Society.

3. Bulletin, "Historical Sketch, The United Baptist Church John Clarke Memorial, Founded 1638, Newport, Rhode Island" (unpublished church bulletin, Historical Tracts, 1965), pp. 1–2. Hereafter cited as Bulletin, "Historical Sketch."
Minutes of the Eighty-second Anniversary of the Warren Baptist Association, Sept. 12–13 (Providence: Printed by H.H. Brown, 1849), pp. 11, 13–15. A committee appointed by Warren Baptist Association at its annual meeting in 1848, reported at the following annual meeting at Pawtuxet on Sept. 12–13, 1849, the following conclusion: "From this investigation, your committee are of the opinion that the Church at Newport was formed certainly before the first of May, 1639, and probably, on the 7th of March, 1638."

4. Bulletin, "Historical Sketch," pp. 1–2.

5. Callender, *Historical Discourse*, p. 62.

6. Winthrop's *Journal*, I:299.

7. Ibid., 330–31.

8. Ibid.

9. Chapin, *History of Rhode Island*, II:85.

10. Ibid.; Battis, *Saints and Sectaries*, p. 325.

11. Winthrop's *Journal*, I:292. The same beliefs and practices were manifested by Clarke to the Massachusetts General Court in 1651, except, perhaps, the claim "justification before faith," which Winthrop did not fully explain; Clarke, *Ill Newes*, pp. 30–32.

12. Ibid.

13. Bartlett, *Records of Rhode Island*, I:92, 104.

14. Ibid. In connection with Lenthal, Chapin says that Callender seems to have had access to records, which have since disappeared; ibid., II:105–106.

15. Hanserd Knollys, *The Shining of a Flaming Fire in Zion;...A Moderate Answer unto Dr. Baswick's Book; Called Independency not Gods Ordinance...*(London: Printed by Jane Coe, 1645), pp. 16–17. Hereafter cited as Knollys, *Moderate Answer.*

16. William Kiffin, *The Life and Death of that Old Disciple of Jesus Christ, and Eminent Minister of the Gospel, Mr. Hanserd Knollys, Who Died in the Ninety-Third Year of His Age* (London: Published by E. Huntington, 1812), pp. 4, 16–17, 20, 23, 26. Hereafter cited as Kiffin, *Hanserd Knollys.*
Kiffin knew Knollys from 1637–91; Kiffin could have baptized Knollys while Knollys was awaiting passage to America, from 1636–38.

17. William Buell Sprague, *Annals of the American Baptist Pulpit...*(9 vols., New York: Robert Carter & Brothers, 1860) VI:7.
Clarke cited Knollys in his letter to Robert Bennett on August 25, 1655; Barrie White, "John Clarke to Robert Bennett, 25th August 1655," *Baptist Quarterly* (October 1977), 142–44.

18. Backus, *History of the Baptists*, I:82–3, footnotes.

19. Kiffin, *Hanserd Knollys*, pp. 26–8.

20. Lechford, *Plain Dealing*, III:98–99.
Although this suggests that Knollys was a Baptist at the time, the baptismal mode was not stated. Since no record has been produced to show that Knollys was immersed between 1638 and 1641, or after he returned to England, Knollys must have been immersed while awaiting passage to America?

21. Kiffin, *Hanserd Knollys*, pp. 5, 6, 31, 33–4.

22. Knollys, *Moderate Answer.*

23. James Kenworthy, *History of the Baptist Church at Hill Cliffe*, 1882, p. 47. Kenworthy was pastor of Hill Cliffe at the time he wrote this work.
This paper, in the form of a dissertation, is on microfilm at Southwestern Baptist Seminary, Fort Worth, Texas. It suggests contact with the Particular Baptists of London through Hanserd Knollys' correspondence with Hill Cliffe in June of 1654.

24. Alfred Clair Underwood, *A History of the English Baptists* (London: The Carey Kingsgate Press, 1961) p. 61; Kiffin, *Hanserd Knollys*, p. 35. British Baptist author Underwood probably based his claim on a manifesto that appeared with Knollys' name and "other godly and peaceable persons" who were charged and arrested for connections with Venner and Fifth Monarchy in 1660.

25. Samuel R. Gardiner, *The History of the Great Civil War 1642–1649* (3 vols., London: Longmans, Green and Co., 1889) II:307.

26. John Mockett Cramp, *Baptist History: from the Foundation of the Christian Church to the close of the Eighteenth century* (Philadelphia: American Baptist Publication Society, 1869) p. 440. Hereafter cited as Cramp, *Baptist History*

27. Knollys, *Moderate Answer*, pp. 9, 11, 15; Cramp, *Baptist History*, pp. 437–38, 442–43.
On one occasion, Knollys called for Elders William Kiffin and Vavasor Powell to pray for him after two trained physicians failed to help him. When Elder Benjamin Keach became deathly ill, Knollys prayed that God would extend his life fifteen years, and Knollys claimed it was granted.

28. Lechford, *Plain Dealing*, pp. 96–7, 402–3; a corrected quotation, based on the cited manuscript entries; ibid., pp. 402–403.

29. Ibid.

30. Winthrop's *Journal*, II:41.

31. Richard M. Bayles ed. *History of Newport County, Rhode Island. From the Year 1638 to the Year 1887, Including the Settlement of Its Towns, and their Subsequent Progress* (New York: L.E. Preston & Co., 1888), p. 152.

32. Winthrop's *Journal*, II:39. Evidently, the Hutchinson faction adopted some of Roger Williams's ideas; like Williams, the group may have adopted the Seeker position. Cf. Bartlett, *Letters of Roger Williams, passim.*

33. Clarke, *Ill Newes*, 31. This indicates the confusion of the Puritan Elders over the prevailing differences of opinion, and it seems they knew less about the notions of those in Rhode Island than some have imagined.

34. Bartlett, *Records of Rhode Island*, I:*passim*.

35. Edwards, *Materials*, p. 302. Editor Samuel L. Caldwell listed basically the same citation; cf. Caldwell ed. *The Bloody Tenent Yet More Bloody*; In *The Complete Writings of Roger Williams*, IV:55.

36. A thrust aimed at the Puritan churches of the Bay.

37. Clarke, "To the true Christian Reader"; *Ill Newes*, pp.19–20. This was aimed at the Hutchinson faction, Quakerism and Roger Williams and his "Seeker" position.

38. Comfort Edwin Barrows ed. *The Diary of John Comer*; In *Collections of the Rhode Island Historical Society* (Providence: Published for the Society, 1893) VIII:25. Hereafter cited as Comer, *Diary*.

39. Callender, *Historical Discourse*, p. 63. Relative to the early disposition of the church, Callender, most often is the source cited. His list differs from Edwards's only in that Callender leaves off the two wives. In former pastor Wilbur Cheesman Nelson's list, Thomas Painter appears, and Nelson cites all fifteen names. Cf. Nelson, *Hero of Aquidneck, Life of Dr. John Clarke* (Bloomfield, New Jersey: Schaefer Enterprises, 1938), p. 70.

40. Edwards, *Materials*, pp. 313–4.

41. Ibid., p. 324. Edwards may be mistaken in the date of 1644; if so, he left out some of the members. More importantly, he omitted Samuel Hubbard who compiled the list of 1648.

42. Bulletin, "Historical Sketch," p. 3.

43. George Augustus Lofton, *Defense of the Jessey Records and Kiffin Manuscript with a Review of Dr. John T. Christian's Work Entitled: "Baptist History Vindicated"* (Nashville: Marshall and Bruce, 1899), pp. 188–89, 155. Hereafter cited as Lofton, *Review of the Question*.

44. William Thomas Whitley, "The Revival of Immersion in Holland and England," *Transactions of the Baptist Historical Society* (May 1912) I:31–5. Hereafter cited as *Transactions*. Cyril Lucar sent to London the famous Alexandrian manuscript of the Septuagint and of the New Testament, presently housed in the British Museum.

45. W. T. Whitley, *Baptists of London 1612–1928* (London: Carey Kingsgate Press, 1928), p. 105.

46. W. C. Nelson, "Dr. John Clarke and the Baptist Beginnings in Newport," *Bulletin of the Newport Historical Society*, No. 101, Newport (January 1940), Religious Services During Newport Tercentenary—Annual Reports, pp. 43–4. Isaac Backus pastored such a church in 1776, and Hanserd Knollys seemed to have organized a similar group as well.

47. At that time, Knollys looked upon any church/state structure as worldly and not according to the pattern of New Testament practice. Of course, some Baptist ministers in London were public servants such as Henry Jessey, William Kiffin, and others. Cf. British State Papers.

48. Nelson, "Dr. John Clarke and the Baptist Beginnings in Newport," pp. 43–4.

49. Ibid. Dale Miller affirmed that the church of 1638 disbanded in 1642, but his argument for this was probably drawn from Lechford's work in which Lechford used the expression "was a church." However, this apparent error in the manuscript was corrected to read "is"; cf. above and Lechford, *Plain Dealing*, pp. 402–403.

50. Ibid.

Chapter VII
Biblical Context of Religion

By the latest in 1649 an active Baptist crusade was begun by the Baptists at Newport, Rhode Island, under the leadership of missionary-pastor John Clarke and his companion in the ministry, Elder Mark Lucar. In that year both Clarke and Lucar were at Seekonk, Massachusetts, not far from Providence, Rhode Island, conducting an evangelistic missionary crusade. It was reported that they won several converts and baptized more than a dozen candidates. Roger Williams wrote to Winthrop about the event on December 10, 1649, in which Williams stated,

> At Seekonk a great many have lately concurred with Mr. John Clarke and our Providence men about the point of a new Baptism, and the manner by dipping; and Mr. John Clarke hath been there lately (and Mr. Lucar) and hath dipped them. I believe their practice comes nearer the first practice of our great Founder Christ Jesus; then other practices of religion do.[1]

The expression "a new baptism" sparked controversial notions. As understood by Winthrop, it seemed that the new baptism had to do with one performed in a different manner and for a different purpose than the original act.[2] To some it was simply a repeated or rebaptism performance.[3] A more probable twentieth century interpretation of the account would be like the following: "Since those baptized had been sprinkled as infants without making a profession of faith, a great number at Seekonk have recently agreed with Clarke and our Providence men about the act of rebaptizing on a profession of faith and performing it by dipping the candidate."

To be sure, this agrees with Clarke's account of his practice as he explained it to the Massachusetts magistrates, when they accused him in 1651 of branding their practice of baptizing infants by sprinkling as null and void. The cause for all the verbal exchanges that erupted over Clarke's practice stemmed from Massachusetts Governor John Endicott's allegation against Clarke when he was arrested. Fortunately Clarke recorded Endicott's charge in his book, *Ill Newes*, as follows:

> You affirmed that you did never Re-baptize any, yet did acknowledge you did Baptize such as were Baptized before, and thereby did necessarily deny the Baptism that was before to be Baptism...And also did in the Court deny the lawfulness of Baptizing of Infants.[4]

As it happened, when Clarke was censured by the Massachusetts Court, his Baptist beliefs and practices were clearly enunciated. His unwavering position on the proper subject and mode of baptism triggered the following heated and emotional argument between him and the governor:

> In our examination the Governor upbraided us with the name of Anabaptists; To whom I answered, I disown the name, I am neither an Anabaptist, nor a Pedobaptist, nor a Catabaptist; he told me in hast I was all; I told him he could not prove us to be either of them; he said, yes, you have Re-baptized; I denied it saying, I have Baptized many, but I never Re-baptized any; then said he, you deny the former Baptism, and make all our worship a nulllity.[5]

Since Williams' reference to Clarke at Seekonk marks the first clear public expression of Clarke as a Baptist, Champlin Burrage contends that 1648 marks the year that "dipping for baptism was first practiced in New England by Baptists." He conjectures that probably Lucar brought the custom with him from the Particular Baptists of London.[6]

Because of Winthrop's choice of words and the supposition that immersion for baptism was not practiced among Baptists at that early period, Burrage argues that Williams himself "was evidently rebaptized by sprinkling or pouring through the agency of one Holyman."[7] Indeed on March 16, 1639, Winthrop wrote of the account of Williams' baptism but he omitted the word dipping. He merely stated that Williams "was rebaptized by one Holyman, a poor man of late of Salem. Then Mr. Williams rebaptized him and some ten more. They also denied the baptizing of infants."[8]

Further Burrage suggests that the Newport church granted dipping to the Providence group. This seems hardly tenable; no evidence has been discovered by the author that suggests Clarke or his church ever fellowshipped religiously with those at providence nor does there seem to be any evidence extant, in fact, to show even church correspondence was carried on between them at that early period. On the other hand, considerable correspondence occurred between Newport and other churches near Providence and even those of like faith and order in London. Moreover the baptized converts at Seekonk united with the church in Newport, not with the group at Providence. Yet the proximity of Providence, it would seem, should have drawn them into their fellowship, providing there was a church order there at the time and that it was considered of like faith and order.

The Second Baptist Church of Newport was organized in 1654; the First Baptist Church of Swanzey (Swansea), Massachusetts, migrated in church capacity from Wales in 1663, and the First Baptist Church of Boston was organized in 1665. A steady correspondence continued between these three churches and the first Baptist (John Clarke Memorial) at Newport.[9]

Pastor Callender was acquainted with men who knew Williams, and he at no time suggested that Williams was not immersed. On the contrary, he states quite convincingly that Williams was dipped when he spoke of Williams' belief about baptism, as follows:

It don't appear to me, that he had any Doubt of the true Mode, and proper Subjects of baptism, but, that no Man had any Authority, to revive the Practice, of the sacred Ordinances, without a new and immediate Commission.[10]

In addition Callender clearly pointed to immersion in his citation of Williams as having submitted to a different mode of baptism when he adopted the "Opinions of the People called (by Way of Reproach) Anabaptists, in Respect to the Subject and Mode of Baptism."[11] From a candid perspective, Callender's statement appears to support Burrage's claim that the practice of dipping was abandoned by the immediate forerunners of the Baptists. At least he suggested this meaning when he raised the subject of their reappearance in the manner set forth in the New Testament. One of two things, then, become apparent: Either charges had been made that the ordinances were no longer valid—as in the case of Williams—or, like John Spilsbury of London, Callender saw no problem granting this was true because Scripture gave authority and substance for the ordinance. To say the least, Callender never spoke of restored ordinances, but he concurred in the belief that they could be revived easily, granting they had fallen into disuse or become void through disuse. He made this point very clear when he said,

There was no Reason, to lay aside the Use of the sacred Institutions of Jesus Christ, because they had been perverted, for surely the Disciples of Jesus Christ, must of Necessity have an inherent Right to revive or rectify, any of his Ordinances that have been misused.[12]

Callender further pressed his point on baptism by raising the polemic question, "Why Christians may not revive the true Form of administring Baptism, as well as the Supper, is hard to tell, unless we make a Charm of the Institution."[13] Obviously Callender answered his own question, at least insofar as he viewed their purpose and design. It is quite certain that Callender understood Williams in this matter because Callender's interpretation is corroborated in several of Williams's works.

Williams believed that a general apostasy of the early churches occurred under Roman Emperor Constantine's innovation of church and state collaboration during the fourth century. To Williams the amalgamation of the spiritual and secular arms severed the direct leadership of the Holy Spirit. This hastened the withdrawal of the special New Testament ministerial gifts—such as the speaking in foreign languages and special prophecies—which were bestowed upon the early church and Apostles on the day of Pentecost.[14] Williams maintained that without these gifts no true ministry of regular church order remained. To him such charisma was crucial, as he said,

I answered, 'Tis true, those glorious first ministeriall gifts are ceased...yet I humbly conceive that without those gifts, it is no ground of imitation, and of going forth to Teach and Baptise the Nations, for, the Apostles themselves did not attempt that mighty enterprise, but

51

waited at Jerusalem untill the Holy Spirit descended on them, and inabled them for that might work.[15]

To Williams, without these miraculous gifts, there was no divine commission to organize a church and carry out its missionary functions. Williams looked upon the apostolic office as an intended permanent function of the church's administration when it was initiated; it was to continue uninterrupted until Christ's second advent. Besides he anticipated an apostolic ministry through local assemblies or congregations. According to Williams's convictions, in fact, the sent ministry of Christ initially was performed in three ways. Basically in his own words they were as follows:

> First, In his own person, as the twelve and the seventy. Secondly, By his visible, kingly power, left in the hand of his true churches, and the officers and governor thereof: In which sence that church of Antioch, and the governors thereof, rightly invested with the kingly power of Christ Jesus, sent forth Paul and Barnabas with Prayer and fasting, and laying on of hands:[16]...Thirdly, Christ Jesus as king of his church, and head of his body, during the distractions of his house and kingdome under Antichrists apostasy, immediataely by his own holy Spirit, stirs up and sends out those fiery witnesses (Rev.11.) to testifie against Antichrist and his several abominations; For as for lawful calling to a true ordinary Ministery, neither Wickliff in England, nor Waldus in France...nor multitudes more of famous preachers and prophets of Christ...no true ordinary Ministerial calling can they ever shew; but Christ Jesus by the secret motion of his own holy Spirit extraordinarily excited, in couraged and sent them abroad as an Angel or messenger (Rev. 14.) with the everlasting Gospel &c.[17]

It was the second manner of a sending ministry—that is, through local churches—that Williams claimed had been violated; he never reconciled that authoritative church ministry with any existing religious group. In his opinion, that was the only way the ordinances were to be propagated, and they had been completely corrupted. Therefore since the initial method was violated by the overriding control of the state—through the nationalization of churches—Williams argued, only one manner of propagating the Gospel remained. As a result, he affirmed in the following confession that no scriptural ministry was then extant:

> How many thousand Pretenders have been and are (Protestants and Papists) to that Grand Commission, Matth. 28. Goe into all Nations, Teach and Baptise, &c? In the poor small span of my life, I desired to have been a diligent and Constant Observer, and Have been my selfe many ways engaged in City, in Countrey, in Court, in Schools, in Universities, in Churches, in Old and New-England, and yet cannot in the holy presence of God bring in the Result of a satisfying discovery, that either the Begetting Ministry of the apostles or Messengerss to the Nations, or the Feed-

ing and Nourishing Ministry of Pastors and Teachers, according to the first Institution of the Lord Jesus, are yet restored and extant.[18]

Perhaps Williams expected a ministry that was never envisioned or implied in the world-wide commission of Christ, according to most Regular Baptists. Perhaps, it seemed, he placed too much emphasis on the gifts themselves rather than on their purpose and design. No doubt Williams was well acquainted with the diverse views of all contemporary religious groups and their claims to apostolic connections. But his understanding of an unbroken chain of visible churches extending back to ones established by the apostles, which had always possessed the power and authority of those planted by Apostles seemed impossible considering his expectations.

Nonetheless Williams's view accorded with the early General Baptists who believed the church was overcome by the "Beast" during the Middle Ages. This conception, of course, was shared by many because the view stemmed from a spiritualization of the Book of Revelation (Apocalypse), a view not held by most modern Baptists, the perception, of course, was espoused by certain European Continental Anabaptists of the sixteenth century, some groups of which led to all kinds of aberrant beliefs and practices such as polygamy and a form of socialism. But, it seems all Baptist movements held that churches could revive the lost commission and ordinances should such become necessary because the Scriptures give them the authority needed to do so.

Williams characterized the fundamentals of Christianity as "six principall Pillars or Foundations," upon which, he claimed, "is built the fabrick of true Christianity: On Repentance, on Faith, on baptismes, on laying on of Hands, on the Resurrection, and the Eternall Judgement."[19] Since baptism was one of the six fundamentals and by conceiving a perversion of the prevailing religious movements in their practice of baptism, Williams was led to the conclusion that his own baptism was invalid. He confessed as much in his letters when he said, "I profess my self unsatisfied, as to the Baptisme and Dipping now used."[20] The following points represent Williams's explanation for the defectiveness of the ministry:

> Wherein hath the former and latter Ministry been defective? I answer, In all these four, their Gifts, their Calling, their Worke, their Wages. First, In their Gifts, for notwithstanding they pretend to the Apostles Commission, and to succeed them, Mat. 28. yet they have never pretended to the Gifts and Qualifications of such a Minstry, nor have they ever been able to clear up those two Foundations of the Christian Religion (Heb. 6) the Doctrine of Baptisme, and the laying on of hands. Secondly, Notwithstanding that some plead their Succession from the Apostles or Messengers,[21] yet are they forced to run into the tents of Antichrist, and to plead Succession from Rome, and neither such nor others which plead their Calling from the People, can prove to my Conscience, from the testimony of Christ Jesus, that either, Christs succes-

sion did run in an Antichristian line, or that two or three godly persons might first make them selves a church, & then make their Ministers, without a preceding Ministry from Christ Jesus unto them, to gather, and to guide them in such their Administrations."[2]

With this frank admission, a confession which placed Williams into a seemingly inextricable dilemma—religiously speaking—a frustrated state from which Williams never recovered. Eventually this led him to become a "Seeker," yet he acknowledged there had always been a God-sent ministry. Notwithstanding Williams insisted he was not completely at peace with respect to its proper church order. Here, of course, it becomes clear that Williams was at times misunderstood and misquoted, as the following confession demonstrates:

> In the discourse it will appear, how greatly some mistake, which say I declame against all Ministries, all Churches, all Ordinances; for I professedly avow and maintain, that since the Apostasie, and the interrupting of the first ministry and order, God hath graciously and immediately stirred up and sent forth the ministrie of his Prophets, who during all the raigne of Antichrist, have prophesied in sackcloth, and the saints and people of God have more or less gathered to and assembled with them: they have praid and fasted together, and exhorted and comforted each other, and so do, notwithstanding that some are not perswaded and satisfied, (as others conceive themselves to be) as touching the doctrine of Baptismes, and laying on of hands.[23]

Some of these ancient witnesses of Christ, whom Williams cited, were the medieval Waldenses; he counted them as witnesses to the "truths of Christ."[24] At times he spoke of the Lollards of England also as representing true Christianity.[25] This led some to view Williams's convictions on a valid Christian ministry as inconsistent with his own practice. In view of his confessional beliefs and practices regarding baptism, Williams assumed that he reconciled them. He did so of course in rather vague language of spiritual metaphors, such as the following:

> As touching the Church, the Ministry and Ordinances of Jesus Christ; I did humbly apprehend my Call from Heaven; not to hide my candle under a Bed of Ease and Pleasure, or a Bushel of Gain and Profit; but to set it on a Candlestick of this publike Profession, for the Benefit of others, and the Praise of the Father of all Lights and Godliness.[26]

It appears evident from Williams's own words that in his second baptism he was immersed. To be sure, he believed it was the primitive mode. A letter to John Winthrop, Jr., on June 13, 1675, strongly indicated this, "How really I could have brought the whole country to have…received a Baptisme (or washing) though it were in Rivers (as the first Christians and the Lord Jesus himselfe did)."[27]

Contemporary witness and former associate of Williams, Richard Scott, clearly stated that Williams held to baptism by immersion. Scott was his neighbor for nearly forty years and, he claims, was associated with Williams religiously for a short time before Scott himself became a Quaker. In a letter to George Fox, the celebrated Quaker founder, Scott characterized Williams as an unstable man religiously. With regard to baptism, he said Williams was "one time for Water-Baptism, Men and Women must be plunged into the Water."[28]

In view of the foregoing evidence, it seems unwarranted to argue that Williams was not immersed. Indeed although dipping could have been a novelty with some, the mode was not entirely unknown or not practiced during this early period, as Burrage claims. At least two noted Puritan ministers held to this mode: Henry Dunster and Charles Chauncy, the first and second presidents of Harvard college, respectively. Dunster would not allow his children to be baptized by sprinkling by the Puritans; he even moved from Plymouth because of this. Further Lechford recorded that at New Plymouth, "Master Chancy stands for dipping in baptisme onely necessary."[29]

At best, the history of both the early English Baptists and Dr. Clarke's own Baptist beginnings appears obscured. Direct evidence that bears on important issues seems, at present, to be lacking, and some unwitting writers have speculated that the only known Baptist on Rhode Island as late as 1640 was Ezekiel Holiman (Holyman), whom Winthrop said rebaptized himself. Holiman left Providence and traveled to Rhode Island as late as 1640, and, according to Chapin, he was the only known Baptist on the island at that time.[30]

Chapin assumed, of course, that Clarke and others were not Baptists at that early date. But by some modern Baptist standards, it is not convincing that Holiman was a Baptist. Even Williams, whom Holiman baptized, did not recognize himself as a Baptist, according to the Regular Baptist order. In 1676, Williams debated the Quakers in Newport; the Quakers in turn charged Williams with inconsistency because he affirmed the Baptist persuasion yet did not identify with the Baptists in their church order.[31]

Although Williams's baptism may have preceded Dr. Clarke's, Clarke's work with the church at Newport stamped his group as the first active Baptist ministry of Rhode Island. The opinions of Williams, apparently, vacillated and the absence of any settled convictions marked his work as passive, at best. It was not until well into the last half of the seventeenth century that the Providence group launched an active ministry, visible to New England at large and Rhode Island in particular. Whether or not an organized Baptist church existed at Providence before 1650 remains to be demonstrated by more than mere tradition. The only active Baptist ministry, in fact, in all of New England by 1650 was initiated and supported by the Newport church under the leadership of Dr. Clarke, Elders Lucar, and Obadiah Holmes.

CHAPTER VII ENDNOTES

1. Bartlett, *Letters of Roger Williams*, VI:187–88. According to editor Caldwell, who took his information from the Massachusetts Colony Records, III, 173, at least thirteen or fourteen persons were "rebaptized" at "Sea Cuncke."

2. Winthrop's *Journal*, I:297.

3. John Lawrence Mosheim, *An Ecclesiastical History, Ancient and Modern, from the Birth of Christ, to the Beginning of the Eighteenth Century* (4 vols.; London: Printed by Thomas Davison, 1826) II:511. Lutheran historian Mosheim used the word "anew" in the latter sense in speaking of the reappearance of the heretical sect of Flagellants. Thus the term is ambiguous in modern thought.

4. Clarke, *Ill Newes*, p. 32. Here is an example of the two separate charges separated by the conjunction "and."

5. Ibid., p. 31. In one stroke of the pen, Clarke articulated the strict Baptist (Regular Baptist) teaching on the doctrine of baptism.

6. Champlin Burrage, *History and Criticism* (12 vols.; Cambridge, England: University Press, 1912; *The Early English Dissenters in the Light of Recent Research*, 1550–1641) I:366. Hereafter cited as Burrage, *History and Criticism*.

7. Ibid. It appears that Burrage overlooked the clear delineation of the two reasons for Williams's second baptism in Winthrop's account and disregarded reliable testimony to the contrary.

8. Winthrop's *Journal*, I:297. Winthrop's statement establishes two reasons why Williams was baptized a second time, the latter baptism sets forth a different design as to both subject and mode. This appears evident by the last sentence: "They also denied the baptizing of infants."

9. Clarke Papers, Newport Historical Society and Rhode Island Historical Society. These papers are preserved at Newport, but some of them are also among the Backus Papers at Providence in the Rhode Island Historical Society. The Backus Papers have long since been published.

10. Callender, *Historical Discourse*, pp. 57–8.

11. Ibid., p. 56.

12. Ibid., pp. 57–8

13. Ibid. Evidently Callender charged Williams with this error.

14. The Charismatic Gifts are included in Acts 2:1–3; Ephesians 4:11; 1 Corinthians chapters 12–14; also in the extension of Pentecost to all four of the ethnic areas cited in Acts 1:8, such as Samaria, Acts 8: and to "the uttermost parts of the world," represented in Acts 13–19.

15. Perry Miller ed. *The Hireling Ministry None of Christs; In Complete Writings of Roger Williams* (New York: Russell & Russell, 1963) VII:172. Hereafter cited as Miller, *Hireling Ministry*.

16. Acts 13:1–3. This manner of sending is not widely practiced among Christians today; the practice of fasting has long since fallen into disuse among the majority of Baptists.

17. Caldwell, *Bloody Tenent Yet More Bloody*, pp. 191–92.

18. Miller, *Hireling Ministry*, 160.

19. Caldwell, *Bloody Tenent Yet More Bloody*, pp. 21, 64.

20. Miller, *The Examiner-Defended in a Fair and Sober Answer; In Complete Writings of Roger Williams*, VII:246. Hereafter cited as Miller, *Examiner-Defended*

21. Ibid., pp. 162–63. Here, it seems, Williams had the Puritans in mind, but in the first charge, Clarke and his Baptist associates. However the laying on of hands was practiced by some, originating in Wales, it seems, but it was the exception rather than the rule; eventually it was replaced by the handshake, which Williams claimed was a Quaker innovation.

22. Ibid. In the last charge, he aimed at the General Baptists it seemed.

23. Miller, *Hireling Ministry*, pp. 155–56.

24. Caldwell, *Bloody Tenent Yet More Bloody*, p. 353.

25. Ibid., pp. 206–207.

26. Miller, *Examiner-Defended*, 152.

27. Miller, *Christenings Make Not Christians; In Complete Writings of Roger Williams*, VII:36. Hereafter cited as Miller, *Christenings*. Williams compiled this manuscript between the time he was baptized and his trip to England in 1643. He left it to be published when he returned to America, and it appeared in print in 1645; ibid., p. 29

28. J. Lewis Diman ed. *George Fox Digg'd out of His Burrowes; In Complete Writings of Roger Williams*, V:Introduction, ii. Diman copied his information from *New-England Fire-Brand Quenched*, Pt. ii, 216. Hereafter cited as Diman, *George Fox*.

29. Lechford, *Plain Dealing*, p. 95.

30. Chapin, *History of Rhode Island*, II:92.

31. Diman, *George Fox*, pp. 102–103.

Chapter VIII
Religious Intolerance

On July 16, 1651, two Baptist ministers, John Clarke and Obadiah Holmes, accompanied by deacon John Crandall, visited the unwelcome domain of Lynn, Massachusetts.[1] The delegation was on an errand of mercy and had traveled all the way from their church in Newport to visit one of their aging and blind members, William Witter. Witter's house was located about two miles from town but not too far, it seemed, for the local town magistrates to hear that three unwanted strangers were nearby. Having stayed over until the following Sunday, Clarke preached in Witter's home to a small group of people assembled for worship.

Clarke took the text of his message from chapter six of the Book of Revelation. His discourse consisted of three points: "The Hour of Temptation"; "That Word of Promise"; and "The Word of His Patience."[2] From the construction of Clarke's sermon, one could observe his skill in homiletics; his sermonic methodology was expository. Theologically Clarke equated "the hour of temptation" with that immediate testing in Massachusetts, through which the strangers would soon pass.

Like most ministers of this day, Clarke allegorized extensively. Most of Revelation, in fact, does allow for a substantial amount of allegorization. But Clarke, indeed, made a rather unusual application, it would seem, when he perceived that the events revealed in the opening of the first four seals of chapter six were already fulfilled. His understanding was no novelty; to be sure, his interpretation and applications were typical of those who conceived Roman Catholicism as the object of every evil pronouncement in the prophecies of Revelation.

Most unique of all, perhaps, was Clarke's interpretation of the events with the opening of the third and fourth seals. To him the black horse and its rider depicted in the third seal represent symbols of mercenary ministers. As "grievous wolves" they made merchandise of spiritual truths, Clarke asserted. The fourth seal, introducing a pale horse and rider, speaks of the dead and woeful condition of the earth, a destruction caused by those previous false professors, Clarke maintained.

Clarke's interpretation of the events revealed in the opening of the fifth, sixth, and seventh seals follows a line of exposition which, for centuries, prevailed among many underground biblical witnesses such as the ancient Swiss Waldenses and, later, those with John Wyclif from the fourteenth-sixteenth centuries. They equated the "whore and Babylon" and the scarlet colored Beast as the Roman Catholic Church and its liturgical system of religion.[3]

During the sermon, two constables entered the house and shortly after arrested Pastor Clarke, Elder Holmes, and Deacon Crandall. The warrant read as follows:

> By virtue hereof, you are required to go to the house of William Witter, and so to search from house to house, for certain erronious persons, being Strangers, and them to apprehend, and in safe custody to keep, and to morrow morning by eight of the Clock to bring before me, Robert Bridges.[4]

Before the three men were brought to trial, they were taken against their will to a Congregational Puritan religious meeting. While the services were being held, Clarke and his companions refused to remove their hats, in order to show their objection of being forced to attend their service. Without doubt their disrespectful action created considerable commotion as the ushers approached them and knocked off their hats.

When the service ended, Clarke claimed, he stood up and informed the congregation as to why they were there and why they refused to remove their hats during the worship service, especially during prayer. Clarke then made an effort to explain their actions. Their presence was not an act of faith because of their forced attendance, and they could not discern whether the assembly was constituted or conducted according to the patterns of the New Testament. For these reasons, Clarke explained,

> As by my gesture at my coming into your Assembly I declared my dissent from you, so lest that should prove offensive unto some whom I would not offend, I would now by word of mouth declare the grounds, which are these: First, from the consideration we are Strangers each to other, and so Strangers to each others inward standing with respect to God, and so cannot conjoyn and act in Faith, and what is not of Faith, is Sin: And in the second place, I could not judge that you are gathered together, and walk according to the visible order of our Lord.[5]

The apparent disrespect provoked the Puritan Elders. Soon the three men were removed to Boston prison and there confined. Clarke published the writ of confinement (mittimus) which, basically, included charges that there were three men found worshipping in an illegal religious assembly that was contrary to the Puritan order. Of course they were also charged with acting disrespectfully in a Puritan assembly, into which they were brought against their will before their incarceration; further they failed to post security for bail.

> To the Keeper of the prison at Boston. By virtue hereof you are required to take into your custody from the Constable of Lin, or his Deputy, the bodies of Iohn Clark, Obediah Holmes, and Iohn Crandall, and them to keep, until the next County Court to be held at Boston, that they may then and there answer to such complaints as may be alleged against them, for being taken by the constable at a Private Meeting at Lin upon

the Lords day, exercising among themselves, to whom divers of the town repaired, and joyned with them, and that in the time of Publick exercise of the Worship of God; as also for offensively disturbing the peace of the Congregation at their coming into the Publique Meeting in the time of Prayer in the afternoon, and for saying and manifesting that the Church of Lin was not constituted according to the order of our Lord, &c. for such other things as shall be alleged against them, concerning their secuding and drawing aside of others after their erroneous judgements and practices, and for suspition of having their hands in the re-baptizing of one, or more among us, as also for neglecting or refusing to give in sufficient security for their appearance at the said Court; hereof fail not at your perill, 22.5.51.

Rob. Bridges.[6]

It would seem to appear by the arrest warrant that the Puritan Elders seized this opportunity to vent their wrath on Clarke and Holmes for their past missionary work in the vicinity of the Puritan Congregational churches. Off and on for several years, Clarke had baptized converts from the Puritan Congregationalists. Since the warrant contained more than simply the charge of frequenting an illegal worship service, but also included several other past grievances—all of a religious nature—this would further suggest Puritan religious intolerance.

The warrant, in fact, contained some five specific charges and made allowance for others. First, they conducted a private religious service. Second, even though the three men were forced against their will to attend what they viewed as an unscriptural worship assembly, they were charged with disturbing the peace of a church service and of showing disrespect by donning their hats during this service. Third, they denied the Puritan Congregational church order as founded and maintained according to the New Testament order. Fourth, they were charged with proselytizing the Baptist way and rebaptizing such converts. Fifth, the warrant stated that the three refused or failed to post security or bail. Evidently no one in the immediate area would jeopardize his or her social standing by offering aid and comfort to an accused stranger, especially one who opposed the religious status quo.

Clarke said they were examined in the morning of July 31 and sentenced that afternoon without producing any accuser or witness against them.[7] Governor John Endicott even insulted the accused and denounced them as "trash," according to Clarke.[8] Following a preliminary examination, the three men were returned to prison. Their sentences were separate and reflected more of an infraction of religious laws than that of civil ones. Did all of this serve to arouse in Clarke a persecution complex? To say the least, of course, their treatment illustrated a blatant disregard for other religious practices by bringing religious laws under secular rule; thus, to the three men, it was religious intolerance.

Clarke recorded that his sentence was for preaching to a group assembled in the house of William Witter, one Puritan excommunicant's house; for leaving on his hat in a Puritan assembly during prayer; for saying the assembly was not formed or conducted according to the New Testament Gospel; and for administering the Lord's Supper to out of fellowship Puritan members and others.

The sentence of Iohn Clarke of Road-Iland. 31. 4. 51.

Forasmuch as you Iohn Clarke, being come into this Iurisdiction about the 20th of Iuly, did meet at one William Witters house at Lin, upon the Lords day, and there did take upon you to Preach to some other of the Inhabitants of the same Town, and being there taken by the Constable, and coming afterward into the Assembly at Lin, did in disrespect of the Ordinances of God and his Worship, keep on your Hat, (the Pastor being then in Prayer) insomuch you would not give reverence in valing your Hat till it was forced off your head, to the disturbance of the Congregation, and professing against the institution of the Church, as not being according to the Gospell of Iesus Christ; And that you the said Iohn Clarke did upon the day following meet again at the said Witters, and in contempt to Authority, you being then in the custody of the Law, and did there administer the Sacrament of the Supper to one excommunicate person, to another under admonition, and to another that was an Inhabitant of Lin, and not in fellowship with any Church...therefore the Court doth fine you 20 pounds to be paid, or sufficient sureties that the said sum shall be paid by the first day of the next Court of Assistants, or else to be well whipt, and that you shall remain in Prison till it be paid, or security given in for it.

By the Court, Encrease Nowell[9]

Clarke was fined twenty pounds, Holmes thirty pounds, and John Crandall five pounds. The excessive fine against Holmes was probably due to his earlier brush with the Elders at Seekonk, in which he had escaped punishment for a similar offense and because he was converted to the Baptist cause from the Puritan order. In fact Holmes was at this time one of the excommunicated persons cited in the sentence.[10]

Clarke maintained that he inquired about their laws before he was tried in order to learn which ones they had violated. Robert Bridges, in turn, replied: "When you come to the Court you shall know the Law."[11] When Clarke, Holmes, and Crandall appeared before the Court to be sentenced, according to Clarke, Governor Endicott displayed a strong spirit of prejudiced intolerance:

At length the Governour stept up, and told us we had denied Infants Baptism, and being somewhat transported broke forth, and told me I had deserved death, and said, he would not have such trash brought into their jurisdiction; moreover he said, you go up and down, and secretly insinuate into those that are weak, but you cannot maintain it before our Ministers, you may try, and discourse or dispute with them, &c.[12]

Clarke was insulted by such degrading innuendoes. He perceived such as a sarcastic defamation of his convictions and well-trained mind; he viewed them as a religious challenge, which theologically provoked to him a response. Granting that this was said in open court, this constituted a bold challenge to defend his faith, as Clarke said. Confidently Clarke considered himself a capable opponent of any Puritan Elder, including John Cotton. For this reason, the next day, on July 31, 1651, from his prison cell Clarke drafted a motion to the Court—which follows—to debate his religious views.

> To the Honoured Court Assembled at Boston
> Whereas it pleased this Honoured Court yesterday to condemn the Faith, and Order which I hold and practise, and after you had past your Sentence upon me for it, were pleased to expresse, I could not maintain the same against your Ministers, and thereupon publickly profered me a dispute with them, be pleased by these few lines to understand, I readily accept it, and therefore do desire you would appoint the time when, and the person with whom, in that publick place where I was condemned, I might with freedom, and without molestation of the Civill Power dispute that point publickly where I doubt not by the strength of Christ to make it good out of his last Will and Testament, unto which nothing is to be added, nor from which nothing is to be diminished; thus desiring the Father of Lights to shine forth, and by his power to expel the darkness, I remain,
>
> Your well wisher, John Clarke[13]

Clarke wrote that the Court claimed they sentenced him, not for his "judgement or Conscience, but for matter of fact, and practice," to which he replied: "I say that matter of fact and practice was but the manifestation of my judgement and conscience; and I make account that man is void of judgement, and conscience, with respect unto God, that hath not a fact, and practice suitable there unto."[14]

At first the debate proposal was accepted. Then, without further announcement, Clarke was ordered released on August 11. Anonymous benefactors, it would seem, had paid his fine. Clarke expressed his disappointment over the turn of events, of course, not because he was so forward to argue, but rather, to him, this indicated that the Massachusetts officials had declined the proposed debate without an explanation. More importantly, however, this might jeopardize the Baptist cause. For Clarke, unfortunately, after returning to Newport, the Puritan Elders blamed Clarke for declining the challenge; to them by absenting himself he was guilty of default.[15]

In order to avoid guilt for the debate cancellation, Clarke wrote another letter to the Court. Again he affirmed his motion that he would gladly oblige them. Otherwise he felt his religious work might suffer as a consequence of their charges against him, granting that he failed publicly to defend himself. Further it seems that he wrote this last reply following his release because it bears the same date; he also stated his intention to return to Rhode Island very soon. This became obvious by the remarks in his letter.

Whereas through the indulgency of tender hearted friends, without my consent, and contrary to my judgement, the Sentence, and Condemnation of the Court at Boston (as is reported) have been fully satisfied on my behalf, and thereupon a Warrant hath been procured by which I am secluded the place of my imprisonment, by reason whereof I see no other call for present but to my habitation, and to those neer relations which God hath given me there, yet lest the cause should hereby suffer, which I profess is Christs, I would hereby signifie, that if yet it shall please the honoured Magistrates, or general Court of this Colony, to grant my former request under their Secretaries hand, I shall cheerfully imbrace it, and upon your motion shall through the help of God come from the Iland to attend it, and hereunto I have subscribed my name,

11th. 6. 51.John Clarke.[16]

Accordingly Clarke hoped that Reverend John Cotton would be the man chosen to meet him in the debate because, as he reasoned, he "was thereby judged to be the man, and best of all approved of by my self for that same purpose."[17]

Since little, officially, was recorded of the incident, it would appear difficult precisely to ascertain what was said by way of the original debate proposal. In addition to Clarke's book, of course, there was Thomas Cobbet's book, *Civil Magistrates Power*...and Roger Williams'ss Letters, which carried some account of the incidents above.[18]

Nonetheless it would appear that the Massachusetts Puritan Elders were disposed toward dropping the matter of debate. Their reluctance to assume any further action on their part in arranging and announcing the details—as requested in Clarke's two earlier motions to them—appears reflected in their reply to his second proposal. It would thus appear, then, that they overlooked or ignored Clarke's previous motion, which he addressed to the Court and Magistrates.

According to Clarke's first proffer to debate, he had complied with their request. Their answer to Clarke however, according to him, appeared more as an explanation than an acknowledgment, which was signed by Governor Endicott, Deputy Governor Thomas Dudley, and three justices.[19] The five officials denied they challenged Clarke to a debate, but they reiterated, if he would petition the Court to that effect, a debate would be arranged. The Court argued Clarke misunderstood the words of the Court. But to Clarke, since he felt he had already made his position quite clear, he viewed the reply of the Court as a discreet withdrawal.

Nevertheless Clarke reaffirmed his position on a third and final challenge. In this reply, he reminded them of his motion that he had repeated twice because of Governor Endicott's bold challenge to him in Court that he could not defend his beliefs and practices before their "Ministers."[20]

According to Clarke, he sent a motion for debate three times. All of them were ignored, however, except for bandying words, until after he returned to Newport. The first motion was penned on the first day of the month of his imprisonment and was presented to the Court at Boston on the sixth day. A time was set for the event;[21] Clarke then framed four proposals, which he intended to defend. They are paraphrased briefly as follows: first, Jesus of Nazareth is Lord over all and must be followed according to His commandments in order to please Him and be considered one of His disciples; second, dipping is the only commanded mode of baptism and to be extended to believers only; third, each believer is free to speak and act in the church without restraint or duress; and fourth, no restraint by force of such a believer's conscience, is allowed by Christ.[22]

A release for Clarke was issued on the eleventh day of August, and even though he implied he was leaving prison soon, his third and final proposal to the Court was written on the fourteenth, also penned from his jail cell.[23] The inhabitants of Newport—in particular Roger Williams—were sorely disappointed because the debate was not held. Williams himself, as it proved later, took advantage of an opportunity to debate the Baptist cause. His dismay that Clarke's proposals were not publicly challenged was expressed in a letter to ex-Governor Winthrop, written sometime during the month of Clarke's incarceration. In the letter, he informed Winthrop that he "met Mr. John Clarke, at Providence, *recens e carcere*"; he pointed out, "there was great hammering about the disputation."[24]

FOUR-SCORE AND TEN STRIPES

Meanwhile matters worsened for Holmes. Altogether he was confined over two months. Even though someone offered to pay his fine, he obstinately refuse it. As a result, Holmes was marched to a public place, the Boston Common; there, in a merciless manner, he was publicly flogged with thirty lashes from a three-braided whip, thus receiving ninety stripes. In describing the beating, Holmes said the man struck with all of his strength—"yea spitting on his hands three times, as many affirmed—with a three-coarded whip, giving me therewith thirty strokes."[25] Although Holmes was denied the privilege to speak before he was beaten, Clarke recorded that he did make a confession, which appears as follows:

> In the time of his pulling off my cloathes I continued speaking, telling them, That I had so learned, that for all Boston I would not give my bodie into their hands thus to be bruised upon another account, yet upon this I would not give the hundredth part of a Wampon Peague[26] to free it out of their hands, and that I made as much Conscience of unbuttoning one button, as I did of paying the 30 1. in reference thereunto.[27]

Following the public beating of Holmes, two bystanders, John Hazel and John Spur, approached Holmes and shook his hand. As a result of this encouraging gesture, both men were arrested and later fined for giving aid and comfort to a lawbreaker. Hazel was an elderly man and—perhaps due to the grueling ordeal of incarceration—died before he arrived home following his release.[28]

Granting that Holmes's account was true, testimony following the cruel lashing seems incredible, to say the least. Holmes testified that he experienced such a phenomenal protective presence that the cutting blows which rained upon his naked back were as rose petals. To be sure, his account of the experience appears emotionally shaking, as Clarke recorded it:

> I had such a spirituall manifestation of Gods presence, as the like thereunto I never had, nor felt, nor can with fleshly tongue expresse, and the outward pain was so removed from me, that indeed I am not able to declare it to you, it was so easie to me, that I could well bear it, yea and in a manner felt it not, although it was grievous, as the Spectators said…I told the Magistrates, you have struck me as with Roses.[29]

BAPTIST BENEFIT

Ironically Clarke and the Baptists of New England had an occasion for rejoicing following this unfriendly treatment. Holmes said, as recorded by Clarke, "Before my return, some submitted to the Lord, and were baptized, and divers were put upon the way of enquiry."[30] A most unusual and gratifying outcome for the Baptists of this New England ordeal was the conversion of Henry Dunster, the first president of Harvard College.

Although some disagreement exists as to when President Dunster was converted to Baptist views, others believe that he was so moved by the beating of Holmes and his unflinching acceptance of it that Dunster became a Baptist.[31] Naturally Dunster was forced to resign the presidency of Harvard. But this he did with good grace. Eventually, along with his initiative and support, the First Baptist Church of Boston was organized, and Dunster became one of its first leaders.

In 1640, Dunster was installed as President of Harvard, the first school of religious training in the New World. Initially Dunster united with the First Church in Cambridge, Massachusetts. He lived at Plymouth among the Pilgrim Separatists and had from the outset argued that baptism should be performed by immersion. In addition his convictions against infant baptism were given public expression following Holmes's beating, at the latest, by 1653; because in 1652, Dunster had conducted a two-day debate with nine leading Puritan ministers on the subject. "Believers visibly only are to be baptized (*Soli visibiliter fideles sunt baptizendi*)."[32]

After President Dunster refused to allow his child to be baptized, all efforts that were made to change his convictions and win him back failed. Even the peril to his future and loss of his personal fortune failed to move Dunster. As a result, in October of 1654, President Dunster was forced to resign the presidency.[33]

It was said that Dunster was the most learned among them in Oriental Languages at the time of his election to the presidency in 1640. During its early development, Harvard experienced serious financial difficulty, and Dunster at great sacrifice endowed the college with valuable assets such as land and the first printing press in the New World, all of which Dunster relinquished when he resigned, according to author Jeremiah Chaplin. At a time when his private property was sorely needed, nearly all of it was given to establish Harvard College. President Dunster donated 100 acres of land to the college, and with virtually no outside financial assistance built the president's home.[34] On his trip from England to Americas, Dunster met Reverend Jesse Glover and his wife. When Glover died in 1641, Dunster married his widow. It so happened she had in her possession a printing press, which her husband had brought to New England and which, in turn, Dunster inherited at her death.[35]

To some Dunster was the real founder of the First Baptist Church of Boston. Although his courage and convictions cost him the loss of his stature among his Puritan peers, his Christian posture and demeanor moved others to act in the same way. A good friend to Dunster, Thomas Goold of Charlestown, earlier manifested misgivings about infant baptism and, in reality, became the first pastor on the church in Boston, at its final organization in 1665.[36]

HISTORICAL BIAS?

Following Clarke's arrest, Sir Richard Saltonstall in England wrote to John Cotton and a Mr. Wilson, delivering to them a stinging rebuke for their actions. According to editor Caldwell, Saltonstall wrote, "These rigid wayes have lay'd you very lowe in the hearts of the saynts."[37] For some unexplained reason, the entire account was omitted from the earliest Massachusetts records. If it were not for Clarke's account and the various citations by Roger Williams, details of the incident may have been completely by-passed. Unfortunately very few authors and virtually no historians have attached any significance to the account. Have all ignored the affair as doubtful, unbelievable, or simply insignificant?

To some justification for its absence is based on the suspicion that Clarke deliberately provoked his incrimination. Dale Miller, for instance, claimed that librarian Chapin accused Clarke of visiting Lynn in order to "purposely" provoke the authorities so as to acquire sentiment against the Bay officials as an aid to the Rhode Island cause in England.[38] To be sure, Thomas Cobbet, Puritan church teacher at Lynn, Massachusetts argued this.

Williams cited the unfortunate affair several times; he cited Clarke and Holmes' mistreatment in "An Appendix To the Cleargie of the foure great Parties." Further he referred to the beating of Holmes as "four-score and ten lashes to the body of the Lord Jesus in the suffering of his faithful witness, Obadiah Holmes at Boston, meerly about that point of Baptism."[39]

Very soon after Williams received news of the incarceration, Williams wrote to Winthrop Jr., informing him that he had received news of Clarke's, Holmes's, and Crandall's sentences and threatened whippings.[40] Williams also wrote Governor Endicott, whom he cited as "Major," soon after Clarke returned to Rhode Island. Endicott, in turn, then wrote to Winthrop, Jr. on August 15, 1651, informing him that he had received Williams's letter.[41]

Aside from the letters Williams penned, in which he brought the incident to the attention of the Puritan leaders, Williams evidently used Clarke and Holmes as the subjects of his book *The Bloody Tenent Yet More Bloody*. In one of the original copies of this work, which he presented to Clarke, the following words were penned at the front of the book: "For his honoured and beloved Mr. John Clarke, an eminent witnes of Christ Jesus ag'st ye bloodie Doctrine of persecution, &c."[42]

Following his release from the whipping post, Holmes stated that an old acquaintance of his "poured oyl into my wounds, and plaistered my sores."[43] Chronicler Morgan Edwards alluded to the severity of the beating by quoting a remark made later by Rhode Island Governor Joseph Jencks: "Those who have seen the scars on Mr. Holmes' back, (which the old man was wont to call the marks of the Lord Jesus), have expressed a wonder that he should live."[44]

Despite Clarke's bold and uncompromising religious spirit and the questionable conduct of the Massachusetts magistrates against Clarke's religious persuasion, Clarke never in any way breathed a spirit of intolerance toward others. This was most unusual in his day and presents a disclaimer against the axiom: the stronger the religious convictions, the more pronounced religious intolerance becomes.

The persecution that Clarke and his Baptist brethren suffered at the hands of the Massachusetts magistrates became a lever which Clarke used to good advantage in his subsequent long and arduous task in England for the Rhode Island cause. It very well could be that Clarke harbored ulterior motives in publishing his book *Ill Newes* shortly after he arrived in London. This, of course, followed just a few months after the Massachusetts' episode.

At any rate, the book consists of mixed materials. For the most part, it includes Epistles; a diary; a brief history of New England (her laws and religious ways); letters of a personal nature; legal warrants and Clarke's belief in certain biblical principles.

The first part of Clarke's book contains a letter titled "The Epistle Dedicatory" and addressed "To the Right Honorable the House of Parliament, and Councel of State for the Commonwealth of England."[45] The book combines a spirited defense on liberty of the individual conscience toward God in religious matters, with pleas directed to England's consideration in such matters. Such consideration appears to be urgent and designed to arouse the king's defense by aligning the English as the protectorates of free religious exercise of her subjects, just as the beckoning of the biblical prophets of ancient Israel, Clarke wrote.

Clarke is bold in his hypotheses. In the letter he declares the way in which he believes the Gospel should be proclaimed, and in this proclamation he is just as bold toward the king as he was toward the Massachusetts

Elders, who differed from him in religious concerns. While the letter appears as an apology for the Baptist faith, it seems that Clarke probably intends it as a timely and effective instrument, aimed at drawing British sympathy for religious toleration in New England. As an aid to accomplish his ends, Clarke focuses attention on his loyalty and willing subjection to the British Crown. Repeatedly he uses such expressions as "Right Honorable," "your honored arm," and "your honored selves."

Clearly and forcefully, Clarke calls attention to what he conceives as the necessary separation between the two real administrations of Christ's power as exercised in the world—that is, the sword of steel, "whose Sword-bearers you are," as he styles the magistrates.[46] The other administration he calls Scripture, the "sword that proceeds out of the mouth of his servants, the word of truth." Thus Clarke views "this spiritual administration as far as it concerns the outward man...[as] managed not by a sword of Steel," he argues, but by the Scripture of truth.

In a bold but subservient manner, Clarke sets forth four simple but imploring proposals to the British Counsel of State. He begs the magistracy not to forcibly inhibit spiritual ministers but allow time to minister according to each one's own conscience toward God. In so doing, he advises—even if they are heretics—they merely represent the tares among the wheat, to which Christ referred in his prohibition of their harvest or persecution by the secular arm of government. Clarke then asks that the secular power or "sword" be withheld from use against the spiritual "tares" rather than heaping abuse on them. In the fourth proposal, Clarke compares his majesty to that of a prophetic nursing Father in the Old Testament; thus he pleads for encouragement by the spiritual ministers.

Both Clarke's unwavering religious convictions and his belief in the Christian spirit of forgiveness are manifested in a letter which he address to the Puritan clergy at Massachusetts. The letter heading reads as follows: "To the Honored Magistracy, the Presbytery, and their dependency in the Mathatusets Colony in New England, the Author wisheth repentance to the acknowlement of the truth as it is in Jesus Christ."[47] It calls their attention to the error which Clarke believed existed in their manner of church order and propagation of the Gospel a repeat of what Clarke claims he previously had told them in person during his arraignment in Boston. Here he assured them that he bore no grudge nor held any remorse against them for their unkind treatment; on the contrary, he prayed for them.

The letter above served as a fitting climax to Clarke's encounter with the Bay officials and, it seems, he made wise use of it to maneuver the Rhode Island Colony into an advantageous posture with the English government. While Clarke paid due homage to the religious zeal of the Puritan leaders, notwithstanding, he believed that it was a zeal devoid of godliness. As a result, he defended his motive in placing his persecution before the public by publishing the events for public scrutiny. As he remarked, the persecution was not done in a corner, so the damage, he concluded, was "of no less than of publick concernment."[48] His unchristian reception, which he received, he described as "shamefully entreated." In turn Clarke reminded them of the much kinder treatment and other "curtesies with far greater liberties in point of conscience," which previously the Puritan messengers had enjoyed on their tour through Rhode Island.

In his letter, Clarke unceasingly denounces the Puritan church order; now he places the ecclesiastical charges before the public for all to view. He decries their way as "not the order of the Gospel of Christ," and he charges them with inconsistency in their practice of infant baptism, of merely sprinkling them and for accepting such adults who were baptized in like manner to the Lord's Table yet denying access to the Table.

The firm allegiance of the Puritans to the magistrates in matters of religion also receives scathing rebukes by Clarke. Unreservedly Clarke denies that magistrates in a secular capacity can preside over Christian assemblies; at the same time, they exercise civil power in controlling or promoting spiritual discipline. Here Clarke shows the contrast of the coercive civil power with that of the meekness of early Christians, and he strongly denounces the use of all carnal weapons in promoting spiritual worship of any kind.

Clarke's entire letter appears as a scorching public censure against the Massachusetts Puritanical system and its integrated form of civil power over ecclesiastical liberties. He exposes what he thought were the earmarks of a despotic religious hierarchy or theocracy from which the New Englanders supposedly had fled. Therefore his letter served as an apt instrument in promoting sympathy from the English people at large and the British ruling officials in particular, relative to the political design which he had in mind. Evidently, instead of hindering the Rhode Island cause, the work aided it.

In the third part of the book, pages 18–22, a general Epistolary letter of instruction reads: "To the true Christian Reader." Basically it is a sermon treatise, very similar in content to the one that the Apostle Peter delivered on the Day of Pentecost, as recorded in the second chapter of the Book of Acts. The letter sought to acquaint the general reader with the nature of true Christianity, in that Christ's true disciples will be persecuted. Although His disciples should expect this, they should not despair nor retaliate by means of the secular force of arms. Furthermore in so seeking to walk in the true Christian way only the means of a godly life and biblical order of worship should be employed so as to impress and inspire others. Never, under any circumstances, Clarke preached, should Christians force their persuasion on others nor should they resort to obeying magistrates in matters of religious concerns. In all things, Clarke wrote, obey the scriptures for they reveal both the true and false orders or worship.

The fourth part of Clarke's book, pages 22–6, consists of partly an autobiography and partly an account of Clarke's migration to New England, his short stay in Boston, and his reasons for the Rhode Island migration. Moreover this section contains a preface to the main narrative, relating Clarke's account of the religious persecution, which Clarke and his two companions suffered at Lynn. The main narrative, then, follows these introductory letters of redress and exhortation.

The text of the narrative records and discusses warrants and depositions of witnesses, which, by their very nature, should have been recorded in the Massachusetts Colonial Records, it would seem. These are followed by a sermonic treatise in which Clarke draws parallels with certain prophecies from the Book of Revelation and his own experiences at the time. A narrative on the laws of Massachusetts then follows these other matters.

The final section of the book contains a theological treatise on the Baptist order, in the form of doctrinal proposals and an exposition of the proposals. This section is the longest single portion of the work and extends from page 70 through page 113, to the end of the book.

CHAPTER VIII ENDNOTES

1. After Elder Obadiah Holmes migrated to New England, he remained a Puritan for some eleven years. He was converted and baptized under Clarke's ministry at Seekonk in 1649; the next year he united with the church in Newport.

2. Clarke, *Ill Newes*, pp. 27–8; compare sermon in Appendix D.

3. Comer, *Diary*, pp. 74–5.

4. Clarke, *Ill Newes*, p. 28. Although under arrest and confined for a time, Clarke claims he made note of every detail of their difficulties with the magistrates, including a record of both the writings and conversations that passed between the prisoners and their accusers.

5. Ibid., p. 30.

6. Ibid., pp. 30–31.

7. Ibid.

8. Ibid., p. 33. It would seem that Governor Endicott displayed poor professionalism and obvious prejudice when he called the men "trash."

9. Ibid., pp. 31–2.

10. The modern custom of observing the Lord's Supper among most Baptists is in church capacity or together with like faith and order. Under these circumstances, however, it seems quite probable that the delegation was set apart as an arm of the church due to the great distance from Newport, where Witter held his membership; or, the church at Newport voted that the pastor could do as he did.

11. This appears as further corroboration that Clarke was not identified with the Puritans upon his arrival in New England. No such opportunity to censure Clarke would have escaped the astute observations of the Puritan Elders, especially Winthrop's!

12. Clarke, *Ill Newes*, pp. 33–4.

13. Ibid.

14. Ibid., p. 35.

15. Ibid.

16. Ibid., p. 38.

17. Ibid.

18. Ibid., *passim*.

19. Strangely, no record of the incident exists among the Massachusetts Colonial Records. More about Thomas Cobbet below.

20. Thomas Cobbet, *A brief Answer to a Scandalous Pamphlet called, Ill news from New-England; In The Civil Magistrates Power...Second Section, passim*; Clarke, *Ill Newes*, p. 40.

21. Clarke, *Ill Newes*, p. 33.

22. Ibid., pp. 36–37.

23. Ibid., p. 40.

24 Ibid., p. 52; Bartlett, *Letters of Roger Williams*, VI:213.

25. Ibid., p. 51.

26. The sixth part of a penny in seventeenth-century New England.

27. Clarke, *Ill Newes*, pp. 49–51.

28. Ibid. John Hazell was admitted a Freeman at Boston on March 9, 1637; John Spur became a Freeman at Boston on May 22, 1639.

29. Ibid., pp. 50–1.

30. Ibid., pp. 51–2.

31. Jeremiah Chaplin, *Life of Henry Dunster* (Boston: James R. Osgood and Company, 1872), P. 111. Hereafter cited as Chaplin, *Henry Dunster.*

32. Nathan E. Wood, *The History of the First Baptist Church of Boston: 1665–1899* (Philadelphia: American Baptist Publication Society, 1899), p. 26. Hereafter cited as Wood, *First Baptist Church of Boston.*

33. Ibid., p. 28; Chaplin, *Henry Dunster*, p. 93.

34. Ibid., p. 27.

35. Chaplin, *Henry Dunster*, p. 93.

36. Ibid., pp. 29–30.

37. Caldwell, *Bloody Tenent Yet More Bloody*, p. 53, notes.

38. Miller, *Protestantism and Politics in Rhode Island*, p. 120, note.

39. Caldwell, *Bloody Tenent Yet More Bloody*, pp. 51–2, 519, 524–25.

40. Bartlett, *Letters of Roger Williams.*, pp. 210–11, 213.

41. Caldwell, *Bloody Tenent Yet More Bloody*, p. 502.

42. Ibid., p. ix.

43. Clarke, *Ill Newes*, p. 51.

44. Edwards, *Materials*, p. 367. A comment that Edwards claimed he discovered in a manuscript of Joseph Jencks, Esq.

45. Unless otherwise designated, all quotations and remarks pertain to this letter.

46. Here again Clarke differed from the mainstream of sixteenth-century Anabaptists because the Anabaptists, for the most part, accounted that a magistrate (eine Obrigkeit), could not be a Christian or vice versa.

47. Clarke, *Ill Newes*, pp. 10–17.

48. Ibid.

Chapter IX
Philosopher Statesman

In 1649, Governor Coddington of Rhode Island returned to England in order to obtain a Parliamentary Commission, which would establish him as governor of Aquidneck for life. As a result, in 1650, the Rhode Islanders chose Clarke to represent them in England as their commissioner, a role which was to consume some of the best years of Clarke's life. A year later, of course, while he was at Lynn visiting an aged and blind church member and preaching in his house, he was arrested and incarcerated in Boston and charged with proselytizing among the Puritans. Following Clarke's release from prison, he returned to Newport.

By the time Clarke arrived in Newport, the people in Rhode Island were in an uproar. Governor Coddington had been granted the Parliamentary Commission on April 3, 1651, which installed him as governor of Aquidneck for life.[1] Needless to say, the people felt immediate action was imperative. Thus in September 1651, official William Arnold wrote, "Whereas, Mr. Coddington have gotten a charter of Road Iland and Conimacuke Iland to himselfe, he have thereby broken the force of their charter that went under the name of Providence, because he have gotten away the greater parte of that colonie."[2] Arnold expressed further concern when he learned that Williams himself planned a trip to England in order to get Coddington's commission overturned. Since the previous patent, which Williams obtained in 1643, was only for a small part of the island area, Arnold felt the one Williams would acquire also would be insufficient for all of Rhode Island.[3]

Following Arnold's letter of complaint, the people of Newport and Portsmouth in turn granted Clarke a commission to oversee the entire colony's interest in England. If the Rhode Island dream of free government was to be realized, then the people felt that prompt and efficient action was imperative. To them, the choice of commissioner should be one who represented all the people of the island. As a result, Clarke became the leading choice, as the commission reads:

NEWPORT COMMISSION TO JOHN CLARKE AS AGENT TO ENGLAND
We whose names are here underwritten, being resolved to make our address unto the parliament of England, in point of our lands and liberties, do earnestly…request Mr. John Clarke to do his utmost endeavors in soliciting our cause in England; and we do hereby engage ourselves to the utmost of our estates to assist them, being resolved in the mean time peaceably to yield all due subjection unto the present power set over us. Witness our hands the 15th of October, in the year of our Lord, God, 1651.[4]

Roger Williams accompanied Clarke to England, but their respective commissions and purposes differed. Staples's *Annals* makes this clear in his notation taken from the Rhode Island Records:

> The objects of their respective missions were different. Mr. Clark was the sole agent of the island towns, to procure a repeal of Mr. Coddington's commission. Mr. Williams was the sole agent of Providence and Warwick, to procure a new charter for these two towns. Although Williams and Clarke each had a separate mission, both were part of a larger goal and concern; in effect, they mutually aided each other in removing a dangerous threat to their experiment of democracy.[5]

Plans now were underway for a history-making epoch as the two freedom fighters embarked for England.

In company with Williams, Clarke sailed from New England sometime during the month of November 1651. Both were official agents of Rhode Island, and both were duly commissioned by the people to lobby in the British Parliament on behalf of the colony. The overriding concern of the people appeared to be the autocratic rule of Governor Coddington and his recent threatening move toward selfish power. This injudicious act of Coddington's triggered a protest by the people, moving them to turn to Clarke as their more selfless agent.[6]

As early as August 5, 1644, Governor Coddington had schemed to bring Newport under the jurisdiction of Massachusetts or Plymouth, according to librarian Chaplin.[7] Since Williams's previous commission for the Providence Plantations had failed to provide for the colonists' expanding interests, Newport held reservations about Williams's success in acquiring one that would. At any rate, they thought his design was too narrow in scope, so Clarke was sent to acquire a more adequate guarantee of their rights and privileges to rule themselves.[8]

Upon his arrival in England, Clarke's first concern was the publication of his book *Ill Newes*. At the outset, it seemed, Clarke perceived that the success of his mission depended to a large extent on his ability to win the confidence of the British officials and then elicit their sympathy. To be sure, he acknowledged his obedience to secular rulers and even gave grounds for such temporal subjection.

The letter clearly demonstrates Clarke's subjection to an orderly state. To him the secular rule is ordained of God, but it should not interfere with one's religious convictions. Both the church and the status of mankind, he argues, are "a two fold administration of power suitable to the two fold state of being of man."[9] Love and conscience are emphasized by Clarke as inducements toward state honor and subjection rather than as engagements by force and fear. He implores rulers to distinguish between these two "administrations of Christ's power here on earth" and to leave the spiritual realm to the control of God's Spirit.

Typical of the seventeenth-century writing style, Clarke is quite verbose and repetitious. Nonetheless his skillful penmanship and polemics, along with a clear expression of his Baptist convictions, demonstrate his talents and acquaintance with the social, political, and religious issues of the day. Considering that he lived and moved among such distinguished intellectual giants as John Milton, Isaac Newton, John Locke, and medical pioneer William Harvey, to name a few, tells us something of the standing of Clarke in comparison to his peers in the field of scholarship.

Following Clarke's docile but courageous introductory plea, he sums up his letter in four specific requests, all of which are on behalf of the liberty of conscience. Briefly his admonition can be explained as follows: Refrain from molesting ministers of the Gospel; ignore the so-called heretics, whom he describes as the "Tares" of the Gospel; withhold the secular sword from giving aid "to the beast" (Catholic power); and encourage and protect the spiritual faithful who are good, loyal subjects of the government. Even though Clarke very clearly acknowledges a spirit of subjection to orderly government, he was accused of denying such by the Puritan church teacher, Thomas Cobbet, at Lynn, Massachusetts.[10]

CLARKE'S WIDE-RANGE OF SERVICE

As a duly commissioned agent, Clarke then turned his attention toward official duties. Through his mediation and statesmanship, Coddington's commission was revoked in 1652. Since the inhabitants of Rhode Island still felt rather defenseless against any further encroachments on their new democratic way of life, they in turn proposed to enlist Clarke's aid to obtain a better and more substantial safeguard against such future threats. This, of course, necessitated a longer stay in England than was initially intended. However a new commission was speedily drafted to Clarke. On February 15, 1654, Clarke submitted the first petition to Parliament in which he requested a hearing on behalf of his countrymen. His petition was acknowledged and a committee was appointed to attend to the order of business.[11]

Very little information has been uncovered relative to Clarke's activities during the years 1653 to 1659 except for an occasional letter of State and some religious correspondences. The request to stay in England on behalf of the colony no doubt kept him near London. Occasionally a letter was written to him addressing State affairs; also the Backus Papers contained a short note of a religious nature, which reflects Clarke's Christian hope for the enlargement of God's Kingdom.[12]

During this period Clarke was also active in religious work and perhaps cultivated friendships within the British Parliament as well. Through close association with Williams, Clarke was probably introduced to important political figures, men who later rendered him and the Rhode Island cause great service.

In the early summer of 1654, Williams left the remainder of his affairs in Clarke's hands and returned to Providence.[13] From that time forward, Clarke was the sole agent in England for the island. As it happened, his service as representative proved to be long, arduous, and expensive, a task that required the utmost of statesmanship. Because of Great Britain's instability at the time, the success of Clarke's mission was severely hampered.

Following the execution of King Charles I in 1649, Olive P. Cromwell became the leader of state over a Republican form of government called the Commonwealth. In 1653, Cromwell was made the "Lord Protector" over England, Scotland, and Ireland. However, during the next several years—until 1660, in fact—England was plagued with the Fifth Monarchy, an insurrectionary movement. Moreover certain Baptists were targeted as being involved;[14] this made matters more grave because Clarke was a Baptist. As a result, this combination of circumstances made for Clarke near insurmountable odds.

MISTAKEN IDENTITY

In 1654, the Fifth Monarchy movement had begun an aggressive campaign. In August of that year they issued a manifesto, which announced that regular meetings would be held to discuss their activities. At the time, there were 150 signatures on the list, according to an article in the *Baptist Quarterly*. Among those signatures was John Clarke, one of twelve members of the Baptist church pastored by Henry Jessey, whose name also appeared on the document.[15] As a gesture designed to discourage Oliver P. Cromwell from accepting the title of king, an address was signed—chiefly by Baptists—and presented to Cromwell on April 3, 1657.[16]

An anonymous writer of the article, "The English Career of John Clarke, Rhode Island," seems to suggest that this Clarke could have been the Rhode Island statesman.[17] It would appear, however, that the writer has Dr. Clarke of Rhode Island confused with still another Clarke. Such a conclusion is based on material uncovered in England, along with Dr. Clarke's correspondence and his other duties at the time.[18] The article claims that the Clarke in question was arrested at the Coleman Street meeting of April 1658, but Mr. Jones of Guildhall says "this [Clarke's] Indictment cannot have been in respect of a meeting in Coleman Street which is some distance from the parish of St. Mary Bothaw."[19]

Further Jones could not find an Indictment against Clarke relative to the Coleman Street meeting.[20] The solution to the place of arrest seems resolved by Jones, who wrote that "on the file for the April Sessions there are also two Indictments against a Wentworth Day for speaking seditious words, firstly on 18th March in the parish of St. Stephen Coleman Street and secondly on 2nd April in the parish of St. Mary Bothaw."[21]

Thus it would appear that the time and place of arrest of this Clarke and that of Wentworth Day are grouped together in a confused manner. Also, along with this Clarke's occupation, it would indicate that the John Clarke "rug maker" arrested was not Dr. Clarke the Rhode Island agent. The matter becomes even clearer in General Baptist minister John Canne's book;

Canne writes that he was arrested along with Clarke, Day, and several others.[22] In fact most of those arrested were General Baptists. The *Calendar of State Papers* cited Canne, Day, Clarke, and John Belcher as among those arrested for Fifth Monarchy activities.[23]

DIVERSIFIED ACTIVITIES

Outside of publishing his book *Ill Newes*, one of the first things that Dr. Clarke did when he arrived in London was to join a Particular Baptist church, the one that William Kiffin pastored.[24] In between his duties of State, Clarke was active in the Baptist ministry. Although it would seem unlikely that he received much pay for these religious services, albeit, he wrote that this was "a cheefe place for [his] proffitt and preference."[25] Most of Clarke's big expense while in England was probably his room and board, which his ministry may have provided.

In addition to the ministry, a Warwick letter claims that Clarke supplied legal services, so the Warwick town clerk wrote: "He was much employed about modelizing of matters, concerning the affaires of England as his letters have declared; in which noe doubt he was incouradged by men of noe small estates, who in all licklyhood did comunicate liberally unto him for such his labours and studies."[26]

Further it would seem that Clarke also practiced medicine to some degree in London, but it becomes very difficult to document any particular services.[27] Missing and inadequate records prohibit a complete or satisfying account of Clarke's activities, yet his service for the colony can be traced quite accurately. The first evidence of note that reveals his work in Parliament was penned by Oliver Cromwell to Rhode Island in 1655.[28]

On May 12, 1656, Clarke signed a power of attorney to receive a legacy left to his wife, Elizabeth, by her father. Three different names have been cited for her father's name: Harges, Harris, and Hayes; but neither of the three names, nor the legacy itself in fact has been verified by the author. In the Appendix to Callender's "Century Sermon," printed in *Rhode Island Historical Collections*, 1838, IV:210, Clarke's father-in-law's name is given as "John Harges, Esq., of Bedfordshire, England," and Clarke is cited as executor of the state. A hired searcher in London failed to find any legacy recorded under either of the three names as testator of a will during this period.[29]

A regular stream of correspondence followed between the Rhode Island colony and Clarke. In addition to Clarke's constant vigilance regarding his attempts to obtain a charter, he was occasionally asked to aid the colony in other matters. On October 11, 1656, Clarke sent four barrels of powder and eight barrels of shot and bullets to Rhode Island.[30] The next year, on July 4, 1657, another letter to Clarke requested his aid in a matter of court proceedings against William Harris. The issue was over the mishandling of certain funds, a charge which Roger Williams had lodged against Harris. The money, it seemed, was an appropriation intended for Clarke.[31]

Apparently the Rhode Islanders were unconcerned over the turmoil and unstable conditions that the Fifth Monarchists created in England during this period. In fact, no citation was issued against him for such a posture in British politics in their correspondences to Clarke: on the other hand, they confessed their growing awareness over the trying ordeal, which they had laid on Clarke.

At the same time, however, the Rhode Island colonists considered their problems in Rhode Island so grave that they sought help from the British. This prompted the Commissioners to contact Clarke and express their growing concern over conflict between the New England colonists at large and the Quakers in particular. It would seem the colonies outside of Rhode Island persecuted the Quakers for their aggressive proselytizing. The Quakers would then flee to Rhode Island to find protection afforded them by the free Rhode Islanders. Because of this protection, the other colonists in turn now threatened reprisal against Rhode Island.

The commissioners never acted immediately to this growing threat in a concrete manner, but merely reaffirmed their desire for a better charter and emphasized that it should be one that would guarantee the free exercise of religious worship. Their letter of reaffirmation is quite lengthy.[32]

The strong emphasis on religious freedom by the Baptists had afforded such people as the Quakers opportunity to take advantage of the Baptists, who had labored for this freedom. Now a concern was manifested for a safe way to check those who sought to abuse this privilege, as well as alleviate the economic restraints, which were threatened by those colonists cited; at the same time, the Rhode Island colonists sought a way which would not jeopardize the existing freedom of individual worship. Even though the Baptists' unprecedented freedom was threatened from all sides, the Quakers were never molested or inhibited in their worship at Newport, Rhode Island.

A SERIOUS ASSIGNMENT

With every shift in the English government, a new commission was required. In 1659, Clarke wrote the colony informing them that the names on all writs and correspondences had to be changed. The colony, in turn, sent Clarke a letter, which reaffirmed his status, but since Richard Cromwell's power—the second Protectorate of the commonwealth—had waned by that time, it was never presented.[33]

In the following year, 1660, Charles II ascended the English throne. To be sure, this did not lessen Clarke's difficulties any because King Charles had a strong prejudice against Presbyterians, Independents, and Baptists. Even several notable personages became victims of his persecution, and the Baptists suffered severely under his Act of Uniformity.

Again, on October 18, 1660, Rhode Island renewed Clarke's commission as their agent.[34] Immediately after receiving this commission, Clarke filed a formal petition for the proposed charter and followed it in rapid succession with several others. From January 29, 1661, to sometime during the next year, at least ten petitions and letters addressed to King Charles were recorded.

Accordingly it seems very difficult to ascertain the exact dates of each petition penned by Clarke, as some were dated by year only. Others bear the date in which they were received in Parliament, and they were catalogued in this manner. When no specific date was noted on a petition, it was then filed in the *Calendar of State Papers* merely by year, including any statement or disposition which was appended to it. All of Clarke's petitions were filed under entries 10, 18, and 58.[35]

The above petitions further reflect Clarke's subjection to secular rule; at the same time, they illustrate his conforming attitude toward the King. Following his laudatory respects to King Charles II and his review for him of the intents and purposes of the Rhode Island colonists, Clarke begs the king's indulgence and action in their behalf, so as to secure their continued and unhampered self rule. Clarke then informs the king that Rhode Island officially accepts him and pledges their loyal support to the crown. He proceeds to plead for the king's sympathy and support in order to guarantee their pursuit in the freedom of individual conscience in matters of religious worship.

Clarke's second petition was received on February 5, 1661. It is endorsed in the following manner: "The petition of John Clarke on the behalfe of the purchasers of Rhode Island etc the 5th of Febr. 1661."[36] Of all the ones that Clarke penned, this one is the most classic document. Portions of it have been quoted many times as a means of dramatizing the grandiloquent part which Clarke had in obtaining the first legal guarantee of individual liberty of conscience in matters of faith and worship. These bold letters in the petition stand out as very unique: "...TO HOLD FORTH A LIVELY EXPERIMENT THAT A MOST FLOURISHING CIVILL STATE MAY STAND...AND BEST BE MAINTAYNED...WITH A FULL LIBERTIE IN RELIGIOUS CONCERNMENTS."[37]

Following the above petition, three or four others were filed during the month of February. All of them were catalogued under the date February 5, 1661.[38] Again, on March 28, 1661, another one was received in Parliament with the following statement appended: "Rec. from Mr. Secry Nicholas the 28 of March 1661 with direcon from His Majesty that it be read at the next sitting in Councell."[39]

According to the *State Papers, Colonial Series*, there was a letter which followed this latter petition. It seems that Clarke believed he had done everything he could except wait for a response to his many petitions. The letter reveals his plans to return to New England soon. The first part includes a hearty thanks for what Clarke seems to refer to as the long awaited charter.[40] If 1661 is correct, no further action was taken toward acquiring the charter until the following year.

On May 14, 1662, Clarke again wrote the king expressing his concern over the encroachments of the Connecticut colony. Clarke indicated at that time no charter was in hand or even issued. To say the least, a growing concern over boundary lines further complicated the issuance of the proposed charter for Rhode Island, an issue which Clarke raised. Quite obviously this grievance was a primary reason for delaying the charter because the boundary lines had to be agreed upon and described in the charter.[41]

The above letter was followed by another just two days later and intones an anxious spirit, a pleading soul, as it were, for an immediate response. Clarke, moreover, requests a document that will mutually be agreed upon between Rhode Island and Connecticut.[42]

The final concerted effort brought results. A charter was drawn up for Rhode Island, but it was the next year—on July 8, 1663—before the long awaited patent was passed under King Charles's seal. To the Rhode Islanders, the patent was a grandiose document and proved to be worth the waiting. It seemed that the most overriding concern behind the king's decision was the determination of the precise boundary line between Connecticut and Rhode Island. In April of 1663, Clarke and John Winthrop, Jr. signed an official document in which both concurred that the Pawcatuck River would constitute the boundary between Connecticut and that of Rhode Island.[43]

Just three months and one day after this agreement was documented, a charter was officially granted to the colony of Rhode Island and Providence Plantations. It was the most liberal patent ever handed down by a monarch up to that time, and its provisions and guarantees were so effective that the charter endowed Rhode Island with the necessary security to progress as an autonomous colony.

The document's precision and provisions were such that the charter remained in force for 180 years. Colonial boundaries were outlined; provisions were put in place for a military organization and the prosecution of war; New England coastal fishing privileges were secured; arrangements were made for appeals to England; and provisions were established for other significant grants and privileges. The charter outlined a form of government which, in many respects, bore similarity to that which remained in force in the colony until the Federal Constitution was adopted in 1843.[44]

As it happened, Dr. Clarke of Rhode Island anticipated Thomas Jefferson's "inalienable rights" relative to civil liberties. From the first settlement of Pocasset on Aquidneck Island, as it proved, Clarke envisioned a popular form of government, a concept of revolutionary proportions among the colonies then and for more than one hundred years after. In Clarke's political theory, the individual mattered more than it did in neighboring colonial theocracies. His popular concept granted unprecedented liberties in religious concerns. Moreover representation for the people and the limit of power to public officials provided a basic check and balance to popular sovereignty. The Royal Charter of 1663 proved to be distinctive, installing safeguards in the election process through the governing body of the State Assembly, made up of a governor, deputy-governor, assistants, and representatives from each of the towns, with each one to be elected by the democratic process.

To Clarke the most outstanding feature of the charter was its impregnable defenses for liberty of conscience. Here portions of Clarke's Second Address to Parliament appear in the preamble, some of which appear as follows:

> Since their arrival there after their first settlement amongst other our subjects in those parts, for the avoiding of discord...[because of] their different apprehensions in religious concernments[45]...and whereas, in their humble address, they have freely declared that it is much on their lively hearts (if they may be permitted) to hold forth a lively experiment, that a most flourishing civil state may stand and best be maintained, and that among our English subjects, with a full liberty in religious concernments...That our royal will and pleasure is, that no person within the said Colony, at any time hereafter, shall be any wise molested, punished, disquieted, or called in question, for any difference in opinion in matters of religion...freely and fully have and enjoy his and their own judgments and consciences, in matters of religious concernments, throughout the tract of land hereafter mentioned, they behaving themselves peaceably and quietly, and not using this liberty to licentiousness and profaneness, nor to the civil injury or outward disturbance of others; any law, statute, or clause therein contained...in any wise, notwithstanding.[46]

In other guarantees, various requests articulated in the petitions reflect Clarke's philosophy and style, all of which suggest that Clarke, indeed, wrote the charter. Included is a brief review of the Antinomian migration; the geographical claims of Rhode Island are outlined; the pattern for their government is given; and an economic enterprise seems to be spelled out adequately. In particular the charter outlines a plan for trade and shipping along with other colonial business pursuits, and there appears to be a well-defined boundary layout.[47]

By Clarke's posture on the rights of individual conscience, he ennobles the importance of the individual as a person. As naval chaplain Bryant R. Nobles astutely observes, "Clarke envisioned the individual as essential in the achievement of the economic goal of prosperity."[48] To be sure, at no time does Clarke ever press for any form of socialism; neither does he ever suggest or enjoin a "familist" society, as did Roger Williams. On the contrary, Clarke views the state simply as an aid to encourage the populace. Of course, he argues, the state should "from time to time give and allow fitting encouragement to them," [49] by which he means the unhampered free exercise of business ventures for the individual's betterment and welfare.[50]

Finally, for the patient Rhode Islanders, under the inspiration and initiative of Dr. Clarke, British legal sanction was granted to the "lively experiment" suggested and pushed by him. He was so honored by King Charles II when he called Dr. Clarke a "Philosopher Statesman." Further the ground was broken for the United States Constitution and the democratic way of life, which did not come until over a century later.

CHAPTER IX ENDNOTES

1. Great Britain, Public Record Office, *Calendar of State Papers, Colonial Series.* 1574–1660, p. 354.

2. Bartlett, *Records of Rhode Island*, I:234.

3. Ibid.

4. Backus, *History of the Baptists*, I:221. Backus claims he copied the document from the original papers. Sixty-five persons (along with six councellors) represented nearly all of the free inhabitants of Newport, signed the commission; a similar one, signed by forty-five persons, was drawn up by the Portsmouth inhabitants.

5. Bartlett, *Records of Rhode Island,* I:234.

6. Up to this point, Coddington was perhaps the most qualified and favored leader on the island; now his non-democratic image was distorted.

7. Chapin, *History of Rhode Island*, I:222.

8. Bartlett, I:229.

9. Clarke, *Ill Newes*, pp. 3–9.

10. Thomas Cobbet, *The Civil Magistrates Power in Matters of Religion Modestly Debated*...(London: Printed by W. Wilson for Philemon Stephens, 1653), p. 9. Hereafter cited as Cobbet, *Civil Magistrates Power.*

11. Great Britain, Public Record Office, *Calendar of State Papers, Colonial Series, Relating to John Clarke,* 1643–1673, CIII, 112.

12. *Backus Papers*, Rhode Island Historical Society. In 1965, the *Backus Papers* were being edited for publication at Brown University. Clarke's mission spirit is reflected in his short letter:
     There can be nothing in this present evil world, so far as I am acquainted with my own heart
     as it stands to Godward, that is more pleasing and delightful to it, than the manifestation of the
     enlargement of the kingdom of his dear Son, and that many obedient servants are added to the
     Lord whom God the Father has resolved to exalt above every name that is named, not only in
     this present world, but in that which is to come; and that they who are so added, being living
     members of that body which by a spirit of life is joined unto that Lord who is head over all, may
     increase with all the increase of God, is the earnest desire and prayer of my soul.

13. Bartlett, *Letters of Roger Williams*, p. 256. Williams' family conditions necessitated his return. His mission, for that matter, was accomplished; the revocation of Coddington's commission restored the legal status of the 1643 patent. Ibid., p. 257.

14. Anonymous, "The English Career of John Clarke, Rhode Island," *The Baptist Quarterly* (1923), I:370–71.

15. Great Britain, Corporation of London, *Seventeenth Century Sessions Files, Calendar for the Sessions* April 21, 1658, Relating to John Clarke.

16. Ibid.

17. Anonymous, "English Career of John Clarke," *The Baptist Quarterly*, I:370–71.

18. Letter, P. E. Jones, Deputy Keeper of the Records, Guildhall, London, to author, September 6, 1965; Great Britain, Corporation of London, *Seventeenth Century Sessions Files, Calendar for the Sessions* April 21, 1658–1659, Relating to John Clarke. The Poultry Compter was one of the city prisons where the above Clarke was incarcerated: "John Clarke brought from Poultry Compter being committed for seditious words."
     John Clarke, late of London rug maker, was charged with having spoken seditious words
     against the Protector on 2nd April in the Parish of St. Mary Bothaw in the ward of
     Dowgate...seditious words, to wit The Protectors power is not of God And that he (i.e., Clarke)
     is called from the Lord to speak against this government and that this Government is not of God,
     falsely devilishly maliciously and seditiously in the presence and hearing of very many people
     then and there present did speak utter publish and with a loud voice pronounce To the intent
     that the true and faithful people of the commonwealth should withhold and withdraw their
     cordial love due fidelity and obedience from his Highness the said Lord Protector To the great
     disgrace scandal reproach and contempt of the said Lord Protector to the great disturbance of the
     public peace To the evil example of all others in the like case offending And against the public
     peace.

19. Ibid.

20. Ibid.

21. Ibid. According to the article, "English Career of John Clarke," p. 369, Day was arrested with Clarke in the Coleman Street meeting.

22. John Canne, *A Narrative; Wherein is faithfully set forth the sufferings of John Canne, Wentworth Day, John Clarke, John Belcher, John Ricard, Robert Boggis, Peter Kidd, Richard Bryenton, and George Strange, called (as their News Book saith) Fift Monarchy Men* (London: Printed in the Year 1658). Canne gives the names and a short account of their arrest—along with a plea of their innocence. While it seems that most of these men were General Baptists, Belcher joined the Regular Baptist church at Newport in 1668, by letter from the Bell Lane Baptist Church in London. In 1671, he led a group out of the church at Newport and formed the first Seventh-Day Baptist Church in America. The group included Stephen Mumford, who picked up his ideas while in England; Samuel Hubbard, who left the Puritans in Connecticut and joined the Baptists at Newport; and William Hiscox.

23. Corporation of London, *Seventeenth Century Sessions Files, Calendar for the Sessions* April 21, 1658–1659, Relating to John Clarke.

24. Cobbet, *Civil Magistrate's Power*, 2nd Sect., p. 38. A conclusion drawn from Cobbet's reference to Clarke's association with William Kiffin, together with Obadiah Holmes's letter to the Particular Baptist of London in 1651.

25. Bartlett, *Records of Rhode Island*, II:79. This notation appears in a letter, which the Warwick town clerk, Edmund Calverly, wrote on December 12, 1664, to the governor and officials of Rhode Island.

26. Ibid.

27. This statement is based on the frequent signature of "John Clarke, physician," which appears on numerous documents and pieces of correspondence, both by Clarke himself and those who wrote to him and about him, including different officials in both England and New England.

28. Thomas Carlyle ed. *Oliver Cromwell Letters and Speeches* (3 vols.; London: Chapman and Hall, Limited, 1905, III, 404. England was experiencing some difficulty with France at that time, which did not cease until October 1655.

29. Letter, Mary Flower, to author, February 3, 1966.

30. Bartlett, *Records of Rhode Island*, I:328, 331, 346.

31. Ibid.

32. Callender, *Historical Discourses*, pp. 234–37.

33. Bartlett, *Records of Rhode Island*, I:414, 416.

34. Callender, *Historical Discourses*, IV:239–40.

35. Great Britain, Public Record Office, *Calendar of State Papers, Colonial Series*, C.O. 1/15., No. 4. This one appears in the State Records undated; cf. Bartlett, *Records of Rhode Island*, I:489–93.

36. Ibid., C.O. 1/15., No. 6. Another petition similar to this one bears the same endorsement and date but is catalogued under C.O. 1/15., No. 6.1. It is longer, however, than No. 6.

37. The upper case type letters are chiseled in marble in modern spelling over the portico on the south facade of Rhode Island's State Capitol in Providence. They are the immortal words authored by Dr. Clarke and were incorporated into the state charter in its final draft and since have become revered by the state of R.I.
There is some difference in the wording of this petition and others, which has been identified as the Second Address. The solution, it seems, is that the two others catalogued under C.O. 1/15., No. 6.1., and No. 7, were originally classed as part of this one.

38. Letters, Mary Flower, London, to author, Nov.-Dec., 1965.

39. Great Britain, Public Record Office, *Calendar of State Papers, Colonial Series*, C.O. 1/15., No.34. The wording in this letter is nearly identical to the first one filed on January 29, 1661, but in a different handwriting.

40. *Calendar of State Papers, Colonial Series*, C.O. 1/15., No. 35. The letter is in Clarke's handwriting and very legible. Here, it seems that Clarke has reference to the charter. The letter was penned in 1662, after Clarke was notified that one was in preparation. However, according to the *State Papers*, this is a letter of thanks written on March 28, 1661. Again, there is a question mark by the date, so this may be an error. The anonymous author of the article, "English Career of John Clarke," believed the date of 1661 to be correct, and he conjectured that Clarke was back in Rhode Island for a short time.

41. John Winthrop, Jr., was an agent for Connecticut. This grievance was a primary reason for delaying the charter; boundary lines had to be described in the charter. Great Britain, Bodleian Library, Oxford, England, *MS. Clarendon*, 76, fos. 255r., May 14, 1662.

42. Ibid., fos. 272, May 16, 1662. Both of the letters are in Clarke's handwriting and are very legible.

43. *Calendar of State Papers, Colonial Series*, C.O. 1/17., No. 47. In Bartlett, *Records of Rhode Island*, I:519, the date is blank, but according to the State Papers, the date is written exactly as cited above.

Copied from the State Papers by photostat, furnished by searcher Mary Flower, London. The document is legible and easy to read. Unfortunately, the boundary crisis was not completely resolved until 1703.

44. Metz, "Address at Rhode Island College, July 8, 1963." p. 15.

45. In order to insure a more proper and clearer interpretation, author supplied the two words "because of."

46. Callender, *Historical Discourse*, IV:241–44. The editor of Vol. IV claims this portion is from the most accurately printed copy of the charter, which was copied from *Laws of the State of Rhode-Island*, 1822, under the guidance of Secretary of State Henry Bowen and compared with the original. Ibid., p. 261.

47. Ibid., pp. 241, 246–52, 255–58.

48. Bryant R. Nobles, "John Clarke's Political Teachings: Historical Developments," XIV; In *Foundations*, ed. John E. Skoglund, American Baptist Historical Society, Oct.-Dec., 1971, 319.

49. Ibid.

50. Thomas Jefferson could very well have been moved as much by Dr. Clarke as he was later by the French in his political theories on the rights of man.

Chapter X
In Retrospect

Because of financial difficulty, Clarke did not return to New England immediately after receiving the British charter. Instead he sent the unique document to Rhode Island by Captain George Baxter. The people of the colony received the welcomed patent with a tumultuous acclaim. Mindful of the heavy expenses incurred by Clarke, at the fall meeting of the Assembly the colony voted to reimburse Clark "the sume and full value of one hundred pound starling" in the prevailing currency. The full amount was to be paid by December 25, 1664. In addition the Assembly voted to give Baxter twenty-five pounds sterling for his part in delivering the charter to the colony.[1]

Dr. Clarke's long twelve-year service in England cost him dearly financially. As it turned out, it seems that he received little financial remuneration for his professional services. Only seven days after he received the charter, in fact, Clarke mortgaged his house and land in Newport to cover his expenses and to acquire passage money for his return trip to Newport. Even the money that Clarke's wife had received in the legacy from her father in 1656 evidently was expended because this mortgage, as it turned out, was a serious venture. The mortgage (Indenture) was made between Richard Deane of Middlesex County, London, and Dr. Clarke.[2] Part of the Indenture reads as follows:

> This Introduction made the Fifteenth Daye of July Anno Domo. 1663 And in the Fifteenth yeare of the raigne of our Soveraigne Lord Charles the second by the grace of god King of England Scotland France and Ireland defender of the faith prs Physician John Clarke gent Agent for the Colony of Rhode Island and Providence plantations in New England America, on the one part and Richard Deane of the parish of Islington in the Countie of Midds. Gent.[3] on the other part witnesseth That the said John Clarke for and in consideration of the sume of One Hundred and Thirtie Pounds of lawfull money of England to him in hand at or before the ensealeing and delliverie of these presents by the said Richard Deane well and truly paid whereof the said John Clarke doth acknowledge the receipt, thereof and of every part and parcell thereof, doth heareby arquitt and discharge the said Richard Deane his executor, administrators or assignes and even of them for ever by these presents doth demise grannt bargaine sell and to farmelett unto the said Richard Deane All that messnage or mansion house with the appurtenances situate lyeing or being in the Towne of Newport in New England aforesaid And all barnes stables outhouses orchards gardens.[4]

By this mortgage, Clarke's entire estate in Newport was endangered. The Indenture seems to have been the final act recorded of Clarke's in the procurement of the charter. When news reached the colony about the Indenture (probably by letter from Clarke), concern was expressed openly for Clarke's expenses by voting to reimburse him for much of his outlay in their behalf. Very early the Rhode Island government made an attempt to meet this deficiency.[5]

In the fall of 1663, the colony voted that Clarke was to "be saved harmlesse in his estate." The Assembly further stated that "all his disbursements goeing to England, and all his expenses and engagements there alredye layd out, expended or ingaged...and in any other matters conducing to the collonys behalf in any sort whatsoever; as alsoe for their expences and ingagements, he shall be necessitated yett further do disburse on such account, and untill he shall have arrived, as he sayth hee intends to come next spring."[6]

Albeit twenty months later the debt remained unpaid. Again, following a discussion among the Assemblymen, a further attempt was made to assume the debt by raising the money to pay it. But by June 26, 1670, a deficit of eighty pounds of currency still existed, and over ten years later, on October 27, 1680—nearly twenty years after the mortgage was made and over four years after Clarke's death—Deane demanded a considerable sum from the executors of Clarke's estate. Sadly there is no record in the Archives which shows that the debt was ever paid, according to Mary T. Quinn, Assistant for the Archives, Department of State.[7]

Dr. Clarke spent nearly thirteen years in England in behalf of the Rhode Island colony—from the fall of 1651 to the spring of 1664. For the next ten years, Clarke was very active in colonial affairs, and he proved to be one of the most valuable and trusted men of Rhode Island.

Clarke arrived back in Rhode Island in time to attend the 1664 fall General Assembly. In fact his presence at the October meeting marked the first account of his new colonial activities. Matters that called for immediate consideration were evident; excitement was high. After all the "lively experiment" which the colony had envisioned and explored for some time bore fruit. No other colony in America or in the world, for that matter, could boast of such a magnanimous push forward politically. The note to Callender's work, *Historical Discourse*, puts it quite succinctly by honoring Rhode Island as "the first government in the world which gave to all equal, civil and religious liberty" (p. 212).

Political matters under the unique charter now called for an expanded and more precise articulation of governmental roles and responsibilities. For his initial role, Clarke was chosen a Deputy; he was appointed to a five-man committee, the task of which was to review and revise all laws of the colony.[8] Further he was put on a boundary agreement committee.

The Connecticut colony had contested the Rhode Island charter provision which established the Pawcatuck Rivers as the western boundary between Connecticut and Rhode Island. Moreover the island's interests and welfare were further compromised by a boundary disagreement between them and their eastern neighbor, Plymouth. The committee, made up of Clarke, Captain Greene, and Joseph Torrey, was to meet with the Plymouth Commissioners and work out a conciliatory pact between them.[9] This agreement was so critical that it was not completely settled until 1703.[10] Winthrop's Connecticut document claimed for that colony the land extending to the Narragansett River or Bay, but Clarke's diplomacy had moved him to effect an agreement whereby the Naragansett River should be regarded as the Pawcatuck.[11]

Dr. Clarke was elected a Deputy every year from 1664 until 1669, at which time he was appointed Deputy-Governor of Rhode Island.[12] In 1665, he was appointed to a committee of three: the governor, deputy-governor, and Clarke, to investigate the possibility of developing a harbor for shipping at Black Island.[13] Meanwhile Clarke retained a cordial relationship with King Charles II of England. In 1665, he wrote King Charles and expressed his approval of the king's policy of sending rich coats to the Indian Sachems.[14]

In addition to the recurring boundary disputes, and ever-increasing amount of work was assigned to Clarke. In 1666, he was appointed to a committee on ratification of the newly acquired charter. Particularly the committee was instructed to seek modification of the provisions for the development of schools, for the fortifications of the colony, and for further provisions to accommodate for the increasing trade of the colony. Further the committee was to attempt this modification through the means of correspondence.[15]

By this time, evidently, Clarke was considered the best legal advisor for the people. On October 31, 1666, he was appointed to make a digest of the laws, "leaving out what may be superfluous, and adding what may appear unto him necessary."[16] Also during that same year the General Assembly reviewed the Indenture of Clarke's which had not been resolved. The Assembly, in turn, stated "that it shall from henceforth be deemed (not to be the debt of our sayd late agent, but) the proper debt of this Colony of Rhode Island and Providence Plantations." Further they noted "that the aforesayd Clarke shall be and is hereby declared to be fully and wholly exonerated and discharged of the aforesayd debt."[17]

DELAYED DEBT RETIREMENT

By the time of this action, twenty months had elapsed since the colony voted to cover this indebtedness of Clarke, yet nothing had been done. As it happened, all of the money prescribed for the debt had not been received. In fact there was some reluctance on the part of the Warwick inhabitants to appropriate their assigned share; they felt they had been required to raise more than their due amount. They argued that Clarke was employed as an agent only in his latter years in England, whereas they understood that the overall amount was to defray his expenses for the entire twelve-year stay in England. Besides the Warwick colonists contended it was too much money for an agent. They also claimed that Clarke had other employment, as the clerk stated "in which noe doubt he was incouradged by men of noe small estates, who in all licklyhood did communicate liberally unto him for such his labours and studies."[18]

Clarke made only two personal protests on behalf of the debt. On July 2, 1667, he filed a paper of protest with the Assembly. The claim was considered and a committee was appointed to audit the records to determine the amount already paid on the debt.[19] Clarke was then Deputy-Governor, at which time he drafted the committee report.[20] The General Assembly approved the report and ordered it to be placed on record. That was the extent of the action, however, for some time.

POLITICAL INVOLVEMENT

Quite often considerable differences arose among some inhabitants of the towns and very frequently this necessitated intervention on the part of the Assembly. Of course at times satisfactory results were obtained simply by mediation through correspondence. One such agitation arose among the inhabitants of Providence while Clarke was Deputy-Governor. In this case, Clarke was instructed to attempt by correspondence to persuade the people to settle their differences by peaceful means. Evidently Clarke was successful because no more attention was given the incident.[21] Dr. Clarke was re-elected Deputy-Governor in 1670, and again in 1671.[22] Although reluctant to serve, the next year Clarke withdrew from any further serious political involvement.

To Rhode Island, Connecticut remained a source of grave concern over the disputed boundary agreement. On two or three occasions, Clarke was elected to return to England. In fact, on June 29, 1670, Clarke and Captain Greene were appointed to go to England to defend the charter against the Connecticut intrusion. This was repeated in 1671, but on May 14, 1672, the Assembly rescinded their former actions, voting to handle such matters in the future by peaceful diplomatic correspondence between them and their representatives, thus avoiding a further burden to the king with such matters.[23]

No evidence in the records reveals that Clarke ever returned to England in behalf of the charter and its provisions. It seems rather certain, however, that he did not go in 1670, because of a letter he received dated November 30, 1670, which indicates that he was in Newport at the time. The letter, it seems, was from his Christian friends at or near Boston. The letter was merely a friendly encouragement and some general information on one of their number who was a prisoner in Boston.[24] Further both Clarke and Greene were present at a Court of Justices held at Westerly on May 16, 1671; Clarke was Deputy-Governor and Greene was Assistant.

Clarke's political activity virtually ended by 1672. Up to the last, of course, Clarke responded to invitations of help. He continued to act as an advisor and helper to the colony until he died. In fact just six days before his death he was summoned to attend a meeting of the General Assembly in which they sought "to have the advice and concurrence of the most judicious inhabitants in the troublous times and straits into which the colony has been brought."[25]

RELIGIOUS INVOLVEMENTS

From the time of his return to Newport in 1664, and up until his death, Clarke was the main Elder or pastor of the church in Newport. The church had weathered some severe crises. Without the talents, perseverance, and faith of Clarke the group probably would have dissolved or splintered off into various groups, yet the church still exists today, after over three hundred and fifty years of existence. From its inception, the church was severely hampered by diverse theological beliefs and practices.

As early as 1641, the first shakings of Quakerism at Newport threatened the newly organized group. The Quakers had a disturbing effect on the island for some time. Further, in 1671, John Belcher and deacon John Crandall, along with a few others, left the church and formed the first Seventh-Day Baptist Church in the new world.[26] The church had accepted Belcher by letter from the Bell Lane Baptist Church of London in 1668, after being arrested in 1658 for alleged Fifth Monarchist activities. Belcher joined the Bell Lane church before migrating to Rhode Island. In the early part of the eighteenth century, pastor John Comer resigned the church as pastor because the church did not practice the doctrine of "laying on of hands" on every baptized candidate. It seems, this practice arose among some in Wales about this time or a little earlier. Despite these troublesome schisms and unsettling disagreements both within and without the church, the church remained firm.

LAST THINGS

In addition to his trained talents, Dr. Clarke was a generous benefactor. He detailed very efficiently in his will how he desired his estate to be handled. Approaching his sixty-seventh birthday, and with the possible exception of weariness brought on by a full and pressing life, everyone thought Clarke was in fair health. Notwithstanding, in the calm and serence moments of the last day of his life, his last act proved to be in harmony with the life he lived.

Following his return from England in 1664—during his last remaining years—Clarke served his countrymen well. In the words of professor Dr. William Metz, "He served the community as minister, physician and statesman, as before, seeking constantly to heal, encourage, guide, and benefit his friends and neighbors and the colony as a whole."[27] Now in his last act, Clarke hoisted capstone to his noble life; indeed when he bequeathed everything he possessed to future posterity, he squared and plumbed his noble life.

Dr. Clarke was married three times, but no offspring survived him. His first wife, Elizabeth, was from Bedfordshire, England. They were married in England prior to embarking for America. Following Elizabeth's death, Clarke married Jane Fletcher on February 1, 1671. Only one child, a girl, was born to this union on February 14, 1672; Jane then lived only two months (April 19, 1672) after the birth of their daughter, probably from complications of childbirth. The daughter died only fifteen months of age (May 18, 1673). Clarke's third wife was Sarah Davis, the widow of a companion of Clarke's who came to America on the same ship with Clarke when Clarke returned from England in 1664.[28] Sarah survived Clarke by sixteen years.

Quite probably Clarke felt that he was weakening rapidly when he drew up his will on April 20, 1676, although no one suspected it. Quietly but precisely the way he wanted it, that night "Clarke departed this life in his owne house in nuport on rodIsland."[29] It must have been a laborious task for Clarke to compose such a lengthy document as his will. When transcribed it consisted of ten double-space typewritten pages. Up until the last, however, Clarke possessed a clear mind, which is manifested in his Last Will and Testament. The first page of the will reads as follows:

> Whereas I, John Clarke, of Newport, in the Colony of Rhode Island and Providence Plantations, &c., in New England, physician, and at this present, through the abundant goodness and mercy of my God, though weak in my body, yet sound in my memory and understanding, and being sensible of the inconveniences that may insue in case I should not sett my house in order before this spirit of mine be called by the Lord to remove out of this tabernacle, do therefore make and declare this my last Will and Testament.[30]

Clarke desired a simply burial, "without any vane ostentation," he said, and requested that his body be placed "between my loving wives, Elizabeth and Jane."[31]

At the time of Clarke's death, the colonial debt against him was still unpaid.[32] Even so his estate was quite lucrative. Appraised at 1, 080 pounds and twelve shillings,[33] Clarke made arrangements for its beneficial use through the provisions of his will. He left all of his close relatives and friends substantial gifts, and he appointed William Weeden, Philip Smith, and Richard Bailey as his "lawful executors," unto whom he bequeathed forty shillings a year for life for each one.[34]

ASSESSMENT

Clarke was not only generous about present needs, but he had a keen eye on the future. At a time when educational inspiration and financial help were sorely needed, Clarke bequeathed a large amount of property and collateral. From these his executors were "to distribute the profit thereof for the relief of the poor or bringing up of children unto learning."[35]

Clarke's property holdings extended beyond Newport proper and reached into what is known today as Middletown. All of his estate he left for the benefit of others, and even by modern standards his estate remained considerable.[16] After over three centuries of time, in fact, Clarke's generosity has continued to perform its benevolent work.

The oldest trust company in New England owes its origin to the provisions of Clarke's will and has remained solvent through the perpetual election of trustees for Clarke's estate. Its claim is made through the Rhode Island Trust Company. This company was appointed the thirty-ninth assign of the trust, and the bank traces its claim back to May 29, 1867, when it obtained its charter as a trust company. The Hospital Trust was organized at that time so that one-third of its profit benefited the new Rhode Island Hospital. Benefits for the hospital continued until 1880, at which time this agreement was discontinued; the hospital then was made the company's largest stockholder. In 1960, a report made of the American Bankers Association revealed that no evidence has been produced whereby any other trust could claim a longer tenure of existence. In that same year, the assigns included Wilbur Nelson, Jr. and Louis F. Young.[37]

In addition to the church Clarke founded, his name has been perpetuated in a grammar school in Newport called "The John Clarke School." This is a fitting honor for one who manifested such a deep and contributive interest in "both religion and education."[38] Further the Rhode Island College, now the University of Rhode Island, dedicated its new science building to Clarke on July 8, 1963, by naming it the "John Clarke Science Building."[39]

During the World War II hostilities, Rhode Island state christened a ship after Clarke. On February 25, 1943, the wife of Rhode Island Governor J. Howard McGrath broke a bottle of champagne against the steel hull of a Liberty Merchant Vessel, the S. S. John Clarke, named in honor of the selfless Rhode Island pioneer colonizer.[40]

The foregoing honors, however, are mere tokens of the fame which belong to Dr. Clarke. At one time, an effort was made to place him in the Hall of Fame at New York University. He was nominated in 1920, on the grounds that he was the "actual founder of the Rhode Island Commonwealth." Unfortunately he was not accepted.[41] To be sure, Dr. Clarke was among the first group that migrated to Rhode Island, and he was one of the principal ones to search out a spot for their home. It hardly seems arguable that Dr. Clarke was the first one to bring democracy to the new world by means of Rhode Island. Moreover very early he codified all of the laws of the island as new towns began to spring up, and he brought democracy to the island by means of the first free charter of government, a type of government that time has proven to be more equal and enduing among the people than any other in the world.

While all past attempts to secure an equal recognition for Clarke with that of Roger Williams have seemingly failed, it remains an apparent travesty on history to continually subordinate Clarke's significant contributions to the ideals of religious and civil freedom, along with his worthy pioneer accomplishments in the political and medical communities. Especially does this seem true since time has proven Clarke to have been the most dedicated, selfless, trustworthy, and efficient leader in all areas of colonial development, such as in pioneer colonizing, religious interests, and medical contributions.

Although the scant and fragmentary records of Dr. Clarke as a physician reveal the need for a more complete and accurate assessment, be that as it may, the Newport Medical Society long ago recognized Clarke's expertise as a physician and in 1885 erected a tablet in his honor. The plaque hangs on the wall at the Newport Historical Society and reads as follows:

Erected by the Newport Medical Society
December, 1885
to
John Clarke, Physician
1609–1676
Founder of Newport
And of the Civil Polity of Rhode Island[42]

As a Christian, no serious blot has appeared to mar the name of Dr. Clarke. His only serious opposition was religious and came when he was jailed and charged with proselytizing in the Massachusetts territory, which to the magistrate merely disrupted the status quo of their religious beliefs and practices. At no time, it seems, do the records indicate that he violated his own principles of honesty and toleration nor did he allow his religious brethren to do so. Since the Quakers rendered the Baptist church of Newport much misery and difficulty, this appears significant. More important Clarke remained a stable spirit in all of his engagements. In an age when (to a certain degree) most men blundered, it seems incredible that no serious infraction could be produced against Dr. Clarke.

As a man, Clarke lived for others. Like many men of the past, he was selfless and uncomplaining. Despite his sectarian religious views, he gave more for his fellowman than he received. Throughout his life he devoted his great talents to serving his neighbor and country, and when he was not repaid—even for his actual expenses and labors—quietly, and unremorsefully, he retired and "ate his bread with gladness of heart." The quiet, unassuming and unselfish spirit, whose true religious tolerance earned him a place as coordinator, counselor, and lawyer, indeed, seems ratified by his services and accomplishments from 1651 to 1664. These prevailed and even increased, of course, until his death. He let others have first place when it came to honor and prestige, while he held up their hands. He was a man, as historian Edward Peterson phrased it, "whose moral character has never been surpassed, and his piety never has been questioned."[43]

Dr. Clarke was the living image of his belief that secular government could and should exist in peaceful and efficient co-existence with religion, but aloof from religious beliefs and practices. Still he was a staunch advocate and participant in a well-ordered secular rule. His unyielding philosophy and religious beliefs in this direction have been tested by the stream of time and as yet emerged victorious. To Clarke, like Roger Williams, freedom of the individual conscience toward God is an inalienable right, and he labored a lifetime to uphold this principle.

Clarke was a seminal figure to American political theory, especially in the practical application of the separation of Church and State. From the beginning of Clarke's settlement in Aquidneck, he advocated a political and religious philosophy, a government by and for the people; further he stood up for a distinctive civil and religious freedom. For sometime after his unfortunate encounter with the Massachusetts magistrates, of course, Massachusetts and Connecticut continued to spread their vindictive polemics against such freedom as that expressed by those of Rhode Island.[44]

Clarke's political theory reflected democratic ideals as far back as 1638, in the Portsmouth Compact. Then the "lively experiment" of democracy was spelled out at Newport in 1641; later in his Code of Laws for Rhode Island in unifying the towns (about 1647); and finally his governmental ideals became reality in the Royal Charter of 1663.

No doubt Dr. Clarke had faults. Occasionally a hint surfaced where some dissatisfaction arose. In tracing these scattered pieces of complaints or charges, however, they all resulted as petty grievances or religious prejudices. Some, of course, were attributed to other men named John Clarke. Unfortunately, here again, the lack of adequate records prevents a more accurate assessment.

May history redeem itself, may it be our bounded duty to rescue from oblivion Dr. Clarke's name and noble deeds, which were appreciated by so gifted a mind as Jefferson's.

CHAPTER X ENDNOTES

1. Bartlett, *Records of Rhode Island*, I:510–11.

2. Richard Deane of Islington parish was also a Particular Baptist minister in London. According to the article "Baptist Beginnings in Watford" *The Baptist Quarterly* (Jan. 1976), XXVI, 206–207, note 12, he was Captain Richard Deane, a member of Cromwell's administration during the political turmoil of the 1650s.

3. Middlesex, Gentleman.

4. Clarke Indenture. This is about one-fourth of the entire document. Original is on file at the Newport Historical Society, and Photostat from original was supplied by John T. Hopf Photography, Newport, through the courtesy of the Newport Historical Society. Author has this photostat framed.

5. Bartlett, *Records of Rhode Island*, II:175.

6. Ibid., I:510.

7. Letter, Mary T. Quinn, Providence, R.I., to the author, October 19, 1965.

8. Bartlett, *Records of Rhode Island*, II:61, 64.

9. Ibid., pp. 71, 90–91.

10 Providence *Journal* (Providence, Rhode Island), October 8, 1910, p. 8.

11. Callender, *Historical Discourse*, IV:258.

12. Bartlett, *Records of Rhode Island*, II:96, 139, 185, 222, 242. Nicholas Easton was the Deputy-Governor in 1669, but without informing anyone, he left the colony. Clarke then was selected to replace him.

13. Ibid., p. 125.

14. Anonymous, "English Career of John Clarke, R.I.," p. 371.

15. Bartlett, *Records of Rhode Island*, II:154–55.

16. Ibid., p. 184.

17. Ibid., p. 175. The original rate assigned to pay Clarke was six hundred pounds; ibid., p. 81. Warwick's objection was expressed in a letter written by the town clerk, Edmund Calverly, on December 12, 1664. Warwick was concerned over its own boundaries, and due to the lack of sufficient communication between them at that time they had not been informed of the latest developments and circumstances.

Clarke spent 651 pounds, seventeen shillings and ten pence of his own money. So really, at 600 pounds, he was not being reimbursed for his expenses or paid for his service as agent, along with the extreme inconvenience caused him in the twelve plus year ordeal.

18. Ibid., p. 79.

19. Ibid., pp. 212–13. This had been done several times.

20. Ibid., p. 254. The gist of the report is as follows:

Wee, whose names are hearunder written...of the Committee impowered in the year 1666, to make inspection into the levie of six hundred pounds, made in the year 1664, for the defraying of the charges about the Charter...that the said committee be still impowered to prosecute the same to the extent of their power, formerly committed unto them and in case there bee faylure for want of execution...that the said Recorder, Sargants or Constables, or either of them that shall be defective therein, shall be responsible for such sume or sumes as should have so been levied by them; and because it is pleaded that there are several other debts due from the Collony to the towne of Warwick, and to severall other persons inhabitinge in the said Collony, it is also humbly offered to this present Assembly as a thinge both reasonable and just, that it may be enacted that such demands may be audited, and their accounts being stated, there may be an effectual course taken alsoe for the payment and discharging thereof, that justice taking place upon all accounts, there may be no such complayning in our streets.

John Clarke,
William Harris,
John Briggs.

21. Ibid., p. 255.

22. Ibid., pp. 302, 306, 373–4, 431.

23. Ibid., pp. 339, 456.

24. Backus, *History of the Baptists*, I:326–27.
Letter to Mr. Clarke and his church in Newport: November 30, 1670
BELOVED BRETHREN AND SISTERS:—I most heartily salute you all in our dear Lord, who is our alone Savior in all our troubles, that we his poor members are exercised with for his name's sake. And blessed be God our Father, that has given us such a High Priest, that was touched with the feeling of our infirmities, which is no small comfort to the souls of his poor suffering ones; the which, through grace, the Lord hath been pleased to make us in some small measure partakers of. And at this present our dear brother William Turner, a prisoner for the Lord's cause in Boston, has some good experience of, both of that which Paul desired, to be conformable to our Lord in his sufferings, and also of the promises of our Lord, in the giving forth of the comfort of his Spirit, to uphold us all, for that he is sensible of the sufferings of his poor members, and is ready to give forth supplies as are most suitable to such a condition as he calls his to...

25. Nelson, *Hero of Aquidneck*, p. 87. The trouble was the Sachim Indian uprising, which broke out the same year in the southern part of Rhode Island.

26. John Crandall, the deacon who accompanied Dr. Clarke to Lynn and subsequently was arrested and fined along with Clarke. Crandall was one of those church members drawn to Belcher and his Seventh-Day Baptist views. Crandall adopted Sabbatarian views about the year 1669; he died on November 29, 1676. Cf. Paul E. Crandall, "John Crandall and Seventeenth Century Day Baptists," *Baptist History and Heritage* (January 1967), Vol. 2, 114–15; also cf. W. T. Whitley, *Baptists of London*, p. 114.

27. Metz, "Address Delivered at Rhode Island," p. 15.

28. Backus, *History of the Baptists*, I:348.

29. Clarke, *Bible*, p. 547. This quotation appears at the bottom of the page of Clarke's *Bible*, probably written by his brother Carew because Carew was staying in the house with him the day Dr. Clarke died; Clarke, Will, p. 4. The date is also printed in the introductory material of Clarke's *Bible*. According to the above records, the *Dictionary of American Biography* errors when it states that Clarke died on April 28. William H. Allison, "John Clarke, 1609–1676," *DAB* (22 vols.; New York: Charles Scribner's Sons, 1930). Edited by Allen Johnson and Dumas Malone, IV:154–56.
Further professor Charles McLean Andrews is off considerably when he places Clarke's death in October of 1672. Cf. *The Colonial Period of American History* (4 vols.; New Haven: Yale University Press, 1936) II:39.

30. Clarke, Will, p.1. Copied by permission of the Newport Historical Society, from a certified typewritten copy furnished through the courtesy of the Society. The pagination in this work is based on the ten pages of the will. Original ms. is framed and on display at the Newport Historical Society.

31. Ibid.

32. Bartlett, *Records of Rhode Island*, II:558.

33. Sprague, *Annals of the American Baptist Pulpit*, VI:25.

34. Clarke, Will, p. 6.

35. Ibid., p. 8.

36. Interview, Wilbur C. Nelson, Jr., with author, Newport, R.I., July 28, 1965. Nelson is the son of a former pastor of the Newport church, author Wilbur Cheesman Nelson, Jr. is a member of the church and assistant vice president of the Hospital Trust which represents the executors of 167 acres of the old colonial Clarke estate in Middletown, R.I.

37. Providence Sunday *Journal Business Weekly* (Providence, January 31, 1960), Section B, p. 2.

38. Nelson, *Hero of Aquidneck*, p. 91.

39. Metz, "Address Delivered at Rhode Island College," Title page.

40. Providence *Journal* (Providence, February 25, 1943), p. 20.

41. Ibid., April 5, 1920, p. 10.

42. The plaque mentions that Dr. Clarke signed his name as a physician quite frequently.

43. Edward Peterson, *History of Rhode Island* (New York: John S. Taylor, 1853), p. 72.

44. A separation of church and state was not a reality nor even an ideal among twelve of the original thirteen colonies. Only in Rhode Island was the democratic ideal proposed and implemented. Unfortunately, historians have played down this fact! Although Roger Williams first spoke out on behalf of the freedom of individual religious conscience in New England, in Providence he set up only a kind of "Familist" society, not a structured one with clear organized guidelines on how the citizenry was to behave or to be protected. This was not true in Newport, Rhode Island.

Chapter XI
A Baptist Theology and Church Way

This chapter examines Dr. Clarke's theology (his view of God), his view of salvation (soteriology), his view of the church (ecclesiology), and his view of last things (eschatology). Clarke's doctrines made clear both traditional and unique inroads of theology and church practices. On the doctrine of God, he was considered orthodox; on church order he was unique, as will be shown below.

ATONEMENT

Particular redemption or limited atonement was a descriptive tenet of the Particular Baptists of London, a group with which Dr. Clarke was associated. Like the Puritan and Presbyterian theology, the Regular Baptists with Clarke believed the doctrine of God's election to eternal life was according to His sovereign will and pleasure. To Clarke, the atonement was for believers, as he stated in Article 12: "[to] all that are or shall be saved." To the Calvinist, of course, this means that before the world began God foreordained a sin-bearer—a suffering servant—to be the propitiation for the sins of those whom God chose to redeem among lost humanity. This group styled the "elect," comprise the "whole family in heaven and earth."[1]

To Clarke God decreed that all things would come to pass in history according to His pre-ordained will. He expressed the cause as "none other but his mere good will and pleasure."[2] In this respect, Clarke identified himself as a Calvinist; otherwise his theology—such as "double predestination"—represented a radical departure from John Calvin, founder of the Presbyterian way.

The earliest formal creed that appeared among New England Regular Baptists, that is those who had a direct link to the Particular Baptists of London through the Philadelphia Association of 1707 and following, was penned by Elder Obadiah Holmes sometime between the years 1654–75. The creed consisted of thirty-five separate articles, which detailed the earliest beliefs of the Newport congregation. In the first article, Clarke's theology stands out clearly in the following statement: "All things with their causes, effects circumstances and manner of being, are decreed by God." This decree he lauded as "most wise; most just; eternal; necessary, unchangeable; most free; and the cause of all good; but not of any sin." This decree Clarke defined as predestination.

Clarke did not attribute the origin of sin to God, but like the celebrated Geneva reformer, Calvin, he believed that sin is the effect of man's free will.

Thus condemnation is the result of justice inflicted upon mankind for willful disobedience. Unlike Calvin, however, Clarke rejected the premise that God ordained certain persons to an eternal condemnation. On the contrary, Clarke believed through one's own inherent free moral agency one chooses to follow the path of sin whereby one is condemned through one's own volition or free choice.

In the above manner, to Clarke, mankind forever separates itself from God, unless God intervenes and rescues, which God chooses to do for some. This God does through His Son as sin-bearer for the one who believes. But only when the Holy Spirit quickens the heart can one exercise the will to believe, according to Clarke. Thus God is exonerated from all blame for mankind's dilemma. In addition Clarke accounted that one can be sure of his election in this life but not of his reprobation. As he stated, "He that is now profane, may be called hereafter." An illustration he gives to exemplify this belief is Saul of Tarsus as given in Acts chapter nine.

THE NATURE OF GOD

Clarke held the orthodox Nicene Creed. His view of God was that of "one Essence or Being," One who created all things both in Heaven and all things beneath, yet was composed of "Three Persons. Moreover, Clarke argued, the nature of God's Being is that of Spirit, and He always manifests active control over all of His creation "by the word of his power." Since God is Spirit, Clarke believed, He is a divine personage Who guides "the souls of the Saints to worship the father, as in spirit, so likewise in truth."[3]

To Clarke the Holy Spirit is Christ's "vice-roy here on earth." As Vicar the Holy Spirit's function—among other divine duties—is "to deal with spirits by way of convincing, converting, transforming, and as it were a-new creating of them, and so to translate them out of the kingdom of darkness, in which they are by nature, into the glorious liberty of the Saints in light."[4]

Obviously Clarke's theology was Christocentric. Here he interpreted the Apostle Paul literally; all of God's revelations to man are centered in Christ. To him Christ was the predicted Messiah of the Old Testament and the "anointed one" of the New. Christ, then, he characterized as the "Anointed Prophet," "Anointed King," and "Lord of all."[5]

Clarke accepted the Athanasian Creed and held to the creedal enunciation, "the very God and very man."[6] The affirmation that Christ was both God and man, manifested in history as divinity robed in flesh in some mystical way, Clarke looked upon as the truth revealed to mankind. In effect he stated, "...God is Father to our Lord Jesus Christ; in a special understanding [God] may be distinguished as Father, Son and Holy Spirit, and yet but one in Essence."[7]

In speaking of Christ's crucifixion, as God, Clarke charged both Herod and Pilate with having poured forth "the precious blood of God."[8] Clarke believed that no person, angel, or priest was accounted worthy to make reconciliation for mankind's sins; only Christ, Who made it "substantially and effectually," both on God's and mankind's part. Christ, in fact, possessed both divine and human natures in himself, Clarke wrote. Here he interpreted all of the Old Testament figures and types as prophetic shadows and figures that pointed to Christ. Further Clarke asserted that "God in his Son made a new covenant," a covenant of grace, and those in this covenant are eternally secure. Therefore salvation is based solely on the merits of Christ, he emphasized.[9]

Like the Anabaptists, Clarke conceived salvation apart from Christ as unobtainable, and no one has the power or initiative to choose God's gift; rather it begins with God. The way in which one is to learn of Christ, the free gift, is by His God-sent ministry which teaches Christ as the only Savior.[10] Following this calling and sending through the exercise of such a ministry, lost mankind—on an individual basis—is drawn to Christ by the Father through the Holy Spirit.[11]

ORIGINAL SIN

The human being, Clarke believed, is trichotomous—that is, every human being is composed of three entities: body, soul, and spirit.[12] Like Bishop Augustine of the fourth and fifth centuries A.D., to Clarke the first man and woman—Adam and Eve—were created in a state of holiness, but by willful transgression they lost that state of innocence. As a result, all of the human race became conceived in sin, called original sin or inherent depravity.

Like several schools of theology in the past, Clarke taught the doctrine of original sin. However, unlike some mainline denominations which ascribed to this teaching yet adopted infant baptism (supposedly to cleanse the infant from original sin), Clarke denied the validity of infant baptism. Ancient Bishop Augustine of Hippo conceived baptism as the means of cleansing from original sin; for this reason, Augustine stressed infant baptism.

Contrary to some claims that all those who believe in original sin practice infant baptism, at no time did Clarke or any of the Baptist or Anabaptists attempt to reconcile original sin by the ceremony of infant baptism as a means of cleansing. Neither did Clarke equate the New Testament ordinance of baptism with the Old Testament rite of circumcision, as did most of the Reformed tradition.

To Clarke the condemnation of original sin is abrogated only by a spiritual rebirth (John 3:3, 5). His statement on this is unmistakably clear when he said that all are "brought forth in iniquity, and being born of the flesh to be but flesh, and so by nature the Children of wrath one as well as another."[13]

Although Clarke never spelled out his views clearly on the disposition of those who die in infancy, his school of thought—some at least—perceived infants and "fools" alike as safe in grace. The Particular Baptist Confessions of London, however, allowed that only such "elect" infants die as infants.

HEAVEN AND HELL

As tangible abodes, heaven and hell were real to Clarke. He accepted the literal interpretation of the biblical doctrine of eternal retribution as well as an everlasting place of bliss. Satan, to him, exists as a being who is represented in Scripture as a fallen angel but presently playing the role of "the god of this world."[14]

INSPIRATION OF SCRIPTURE

Understanding the original autographs as Scripture, Clarke believed the Bible (sixty-six books) was "God-breathed," or related by the Holy Spirit through chosen men who were fully inspired and authoritative. As the Bible originally was given, it represented the revealed Word and Will of God to mankind;[15] Clarke interpreted Scripture as "the Sword of that Spirit," meaning, of course, the spiritual sword of the Holy Spirit.[16] Both the Old and New Testament were treated by Clarke with profound reverence. To him the Old Testament records the account of God's plan to redeem an "elect" people; initially Israel was brought forth as a select nation in order to honor Jehovah's name and prepare the way for a Messiah Who proved to be the Christ of the New Testament.[17]

To Clarke the Old Testament system of worship was established to cast shadows that represented the Christ, who—when He came—introduced the better way, the way of grace by the cross, and the sacrifices, offerings, and holy days all culminated in the Paschal Lamb, that is Christ as the suffering Lamb on the cross. For instance the Sabbath day for Clarke was a shadow that symbolized the end of something or deadness, whereas the first day of the week imaged newness or aliveness in the resurrection.

THE LORD'S DAY

To commemorate the resurrection, Clarke and the Baptists at Newport met on the first day of the week in their regular church worship—as the early Christians did, as cited by Justin Martyr, Tertullian, and others—rather than on the Jewish Sabbath day, which was the seventh day, the end of the week as the day of rest.

Clarke claimed he followed with unswerving devotion every religious command within Christ's "Last Will and Testament," as recorded in Matthew 28:18–20 and Mark 16:15–16. Although the covenant of grace doctrine was the principal issue involved between Clarke and the Massachusetts Puritans, it was not the only doctrinal issue which pressed Clarke to oppose the Puritan scheme of religious rule or even his later refusal to align with the Plymouth Separatists. Further, when Clarke separated from the initial group of Antinomians in 1639, it was not merely because of his belief in the covenant of grace; rather it was because of the Antinomian's instability in doctrine and practice. Indeed, this is set forth in his theological teachings.[18]

RELIGIOUS DIFFERENCES

Evidently Clarke did not leave the party of grace; instead some of the chief persons within the original group separated from Clarke on doctrinal grounds. All along it seems that most of the early religious and socially independent agitators among the Antinomian group were religiously unstable. At least this is suggested by their vacillating opinions and imprecise articulation of their beliefs and practices. Only Clarke and perhaps a few others, it would appear, demonstrated convictions well grounded enough to weather the storm of controversies, as it proved later.

GOD-CALLED MINISTRY

Clarke believed in a God-called ministry. Clearly he wrote, "I believe no man is to rush into the ministry without a special call from God, even as gospel ministers had of old, which is the call of the Holy Spirit." The duty of such called ministers, he understood, is "not to deliver a mission of their own brain, but as it is in the Scripture of truth…" Of course it is through the instrumentality of this ministry that God calls men to Christ. Since, as Clarke believed, "none have power to choose salvation," God uses a "sent" ministry to announce His Will.[19]

Clarke expanded on his position of a sent ministry by adding, "Although God can bring men to Christ, and to cause them to believe in him for life, yet he hath appointed an ordinary way to effect that great work of faith, which is by means of sending a ministry into the world."[20] Since Clarke believed the Gospel exists as a general message to all mankind, here it would seem he denounced "hardshellism." Yet, at the same time, Clarke held that the power of Satan kept men from choosing God.

CHRIST'S COMMISSION

The Christian beliefs of Clarke represent a throwback from New Testament times. It was in the great commission of Christ to His Church at Jerusalem—represented by His apostles—where Clarke stood so unalterably opposed to the Puritans, Separatists, and even to the Antinomians. Obviously this seems to be the area in which the Newport Baptist congregation occupied alien ground from all of the early New England religious groups. Such a posture included the Puritans, Roger Williams's company at Providence, the Antinomians of both Portsmouth and Newport, and the later Quakers as well.[21]

NEW TESTAMENT CHURCH MODEL

On the nature of the New Testament church, her constitution, her work, and Christ's "Last Will and Testament," otherwise knows as the "Great Commission," Baptists stood alone. The strict Baptist persuasion, not easily observed among the fragmentary writings about Clarke, appears rather clear in Clarke's own writings. To him the nature of the New Testament church is that of a believers' brotherhood, a regenerate church made up only of baptized believers.

For Clarke the broad guidelines of Baptist belief were taken from both the Old and New Testaments, but for church order, faith, and the Christian life, Clarke was guided by the New Testament teachings—especially the Pauline Epistles—and the leadership of the Holy Spirit. To Clarke and his brethren, the latter: The Holy Spirit and Word of God (Ephesians 6:17) speak of two undeniable witnesses to all things, both material and spiritual. Like the Apostle Paul, the Particular Baptists viewed the Holy Spirit as a spiritual warrior with Scripture as His weapon.

BAPTISM AND CHURCH ORDER

On baptism and church order, Clarke refused to fellowship with any except those of the Regular Baptist persuasion. Since only the church at Newport was aligned with the strict Baptists of London until about 1665, when the First Baptist Church of Boston was organized—by the principle support of the Particular Baptists of London—the church in Newport did not walk in religious communion with any other New England church.[22] Evidently this was because those at Newport rejected all other church orders. While this conclusion lends support to the sectarian view of modern Landmarkism, many modern Baptists contend that no such idea was raised that early among Baptists.

Notwithstanding there does seem to have been some relations between those at Newport and at Providence after the group at Providence was reorganized by three Particular Baptists in 1654: Thomas Olney, Gregory Dexter, and Pardon Tillingham—along with the Second Baptist of Newport, also organized about 1654. Roger Williams's brother, Robert, was formerly a member at Providence; later he is given as a member of the congregation at Newport. But this could have been as late as 1676.[23] Further except for a Baptist church that migrated from Wales in church capacity in 1663—which settled at Swansea, Massachusetts—and those cited about, the author was unable to locate any clear correspondence between Newport and any other church in New England before 1665.

CONTROVERSY WITH PURITANS

Clarke publicly decried the baptisms, ordinations, and church order of the Puritans. He charged that the Puritan ministers were "never baptized with the baptism appointed by Jesus Christ the Lord," and he accused them of "appointing a minstery before [they themselves] be baptized...[which to Clarke] was no better than disorder, confusion, and part of that which in Scripture language is called Babell..."[24] Without doubt this was Governor John Endicott's interpretation in 1651, when the governor publicly—in open court—charged Clarke with the following errors:

> You affirmed that you did never Re-baptize any, yet did acknowledge you did Baptize such as were Baptized before, and thereby did necessarily deny the Baptism that was before to be Baptism, the Churches no churches, and also all other ordinances, and Ministers, as if all were a Nullity.[25]

Governor Endicott of Massachusetts understood Clarke clearly enough, but it seems that he failed to appreciate or respect his Baptist belief.

CHRIST'S GREAT COMMISSION

Basic to Clarke's practice of church order are the positive and direct enunciations set forth in the Gospels and Pauline Epistles. With Clarke such church order began in the "Great Commission," which Christ delivered just prior to the biblical claim of His ascension back to the Father. This was Clarke's rationale for his strict views concerning baptism.[26]

Believers' baptism by immersion was a cardinal tenet of Clarke's church way. A believer, he characterized, is "one that manifesteth repentance towards God, and faith in Jesus Christ...a visible disciple or Scholar of Christ, one that manifesteth himself to have heard him, to have been taught by him, and to have yielded up himself to him as his teacher, is the only person..." Indeed Clarke offered two biblical proofs for his conviction: the commission itself and the practice of the commissioners.[27]

Clarke wrote only of water baptism. Although he spoke of being filled with the Holy Spirit, he never suggested a "baptism of the Spirit."[28] Unfortunately, in his discussion of I Cor. 12:13, in which the following expression appears in the English Bible (King James Version): "For by one spirit are we all baptized into one body...," Clarke glossed over. He merely translated it as "knit together in one by his Spirit."[29]

In his discussion of baptism, Clarke explicates at length on the confusion that arises from such variations in translation and sets forth his own understanding of the meanings where applicable. According to his understanding of baptism and its applications, he rejected the interpretation to be "baptized into the church by [as agent] one spirit," even though this is implied in both the King James (KJV) and Geneva Versions, the latter which Clarke used. He rejected the translation of spirit as an agent of baptism. This point seems clear in his examination of the ambiguous uses of the Greek preposition for "in" as used in the above passage and in numerous New Testament passages; in several other passages the preposition is translated "with" such as Mark 1:44 and John 1:30–33.

Granting that a believer submits to baptism—in Clarke's framework of church order—the next step is immersion in water by one qualified to administer the ordinance, whom he styles "a Messenger of Iesus."[31] New Testament baptism, to Clarke, demands more than just a figureless rite. Its very design precludes an accurate observance of the ordinance in every respect.

According to the writings of Clarke, he believed that the act of baptism requires a three-fold prerequisite: a proper subject, a believer; a proper design, immersion in water following a profession of faith in Christ; a proper administrator, a duly baptized, divinely called, and spirit-led disciple who stands in the faithful exercise of the ministerial office—properly ordained and appointed. In baptism Clarke likened the act to a "dying, or as it were a drowning, to hold forth death, burial and resurrection…into the name of the Father, Son, and Holy Spirit."[32]

Clarke assigns nine basic reasons for his uncompromising conviction of baptism by immersion only. The etymology of the words employed in the Greek manuscripts, he claims, always implies dipping, and he maintains that both the ancient Catholic and Episcopal churches admit to this translation. Such ambiguity in the use of various terms for the words to baptize in the English Bible, Clarke points out, allows the use of any one of three modes: sprinkling, pouring, or immersion. Basic to Clarke's insistence on immersion, however, he calls attention to the manner used by Philip the Evangelist when he baptized the Eunuch (Acts 8:38, 39). Clarke argues further, "Because there was much water there" evidences the use of John immersing his disciples, including Jesus. To be sure, Clarke argues, it would require very little water to pour or sprinkle them.[33]

Clarke writes at length on the significance of the symbolic application of dipping only. He notes the symbol of a burial of the "old man," as emblematic of putting away the "former lusts and conversation." Further Clarke perceives the symbolic figure of a candidate's open declaration in such a mode as visibly holding forth the resurrection of Christ, as well as the future hope in the resurrection of the baptized candidate. This is manifested in the emblem of being "planted."[34]

Clarke argues that no other mode for baptizing than immersion is commanded by Christ in His Last Will and Testament. Moreover, insofar as his writings reveal, Clarke fails to suggest that the mode of dipping was for a space of time a lost practice among the faithful disciples. In fact he seem to imply an opinion contrary to this in the following words: "Therefore this appointment was, and still is, to be performed by way of dipping or putting the person into or under the water, and not by sprinkling."[35]

There is an alarming acceptance within large segments of the Baptist community that immersion was not practiced in New England until about 1644, at the earliest. While certain evidence seems to support this notion, other documentation implies otherwise, as already noted in Chapter VII. Immersion was both advocated and practiced among certain New England Congregationalist Puritans as early as 1637. Separatist minister Charles Chauncy migrated to New England in 1637 and settled with the Pilgrims at Plymouth in 1638. Although he was not a Baptist, he refused to compromise his convictions on immersion, even at the expense of leaving the company of those at Plymouth. This, of course, was after concerted efforts failed to change Chauncy's mind.[36] As also noted earlier in Chapter VII, chronicler Lechford wrote about "Master Chancy…[and] dipping in baptisme onely necessary."[37]

Harvard President Chauncy remained a Puritan immersionist until his death in 1672, even after he replaced Henry Dunster as President of Harvard College in 1654. Dunster was elected the first President of Harvard in 1640. He also adhered to immersion; later he became a Baptist, a move that cost him the presidency, as also noted in Chapter VII.

As a commandment of Christ, according to Clarke, a believer must submit to immersion in baptism upon a profession of faith in Christ to follow the Gospel order. If one fails to obey this, then one is not following the commandment of Christ. To substantiate his claim, Clarke marshals an impressive array of scriptures.[38]

On the authority to act as an administrator of baptism, Clarke again resorts to the Great Commission, maintaining that the authority to preach and baptize was and always has been restricted to the "faithful" only.[39] Such exclusiveness has led some authors to claim these beliefs and practices demonstrate clear-cut landmarks of the New Testament churches and stamp such practicing churches as the true successors of the First Church at Jerusalem and the apostolic ministry. To be sure, such a conclusion could be drawn from Clarke's description of a qualified administrator. His following statements, indeed, suggest this:

> ...But such as first have been taught and made disciples or Scholars of Jesus, and believers in Christ, and afterwards have been baptized or dipped and thereby visibly & lively planted into the death, burial, and resurrection of Christ, are they, and they only, whom Christ hath appointed and the Apostles have approved.[40]

Those who Clarke stamped as the faithful, then, would only be the ones who have been convicted by the Holy Spirit, repented of sin, and submitted to what Clarke termed as proper baptism according to his understanding of the commission and pattern of Christ and His apostles. Certainly the above characteristics represent those who Clarke accounted as the faithful.

Only those, therefore, who follow Christ's instructions as set forth in His basic plan of Matthew 28 and Mark 16 could claim scriptural grounds as authorized agents for perpetuating the Gospel order. Any deviation, Clarke argued, vitiates all authority to organize churches, ordain ministers, administer the church ordinances, and to perform any other particular church function, for that matter. In turn all who seek to change the pattern of this Gospel order for any reason Clarke perceived as "usurpers."[41]

Evidently by administrators Clarke meant either one of the faithful ministers as an individual or as a church body consisting of a group of faithful Christians collectively. Accordingly New Testament commissioned administrators of baptism Clarke labeled as "Disciples, and to believers, and to such onely."[42] To these, he claimed, are given the commission and by whom the commission is to be faithfully perpetuated. Without doubt, it seemed, Clarke meant that a minister performed the ordinance, but whether such a minister possessed the authority to carry out the ordinance apart from church authority, he failed to explain unequivocally.

Based on Clarke's view of the church as a regenerate body and his uncompromising stand that only those ministers who stand faithful to the New Testament order would indicate that Clarke held to the church as a body that extends authority to administer the Christian functions. A tenable solution to the question of authority, it seems, would be that the collective body under the direction of the Holy Spirit—as it appears in Acts 13—would be the direct authority such as those whom Clarke cited as the "Commissioners." On the other hand, the indirect authority would be the minister(s) delegated by such a body to perform a given function of the church such as missionaries or others when it might be impossible for them to receive the required direct church authority at the time of need as designated by the church of which they are members.

Be that as it may, whether the commission was intended for Gospel ministers or a local church, a cursory reading of Clarke's writings reveals some ambiguity. One might interpret his understanding of authority as emanating directly from the Holy Spirit, apart from a body of baptized believers. This being the case, since Clarke did not recognize the Puritan or Separatist Congregationalists—even Roger Williams—as qualified authority to administer baptism; for him this belief would admit to an inescapable difficulty. As a matter of record, Clarke rejected the Puritans or Separatists even as God-called ministers, and the author could find no reference where Williams was accepted as a minister, either by Clarke or by Clarke's brethren.[43]

In at least one instance Clarke cited those initially authorized administrators as "the faithful Apostles, and first Commissioners of Christ Jesus..."[44] Here Clarke ascribed authority to an apparent faithful line, but he failed to explain whether he believed it was an unbroken succession of orderly assemblies from Christ and His apostles or simply groups of Christians who—amidst other rising groups of religion such as the Ebonites and Gnostic elements—chose to denounce every vestige of Christian practice such as holy days and certain ceremonies which, to them, appeared counter to the New Testament order.

To be sure, nowhere did Clarke state clearly that Jesus gave His commission to baptize and conduct a proper church order to the instruction of a local church, as is suggested in Acts 13. On the other hand, he did not discount this belief, but Clarke followed scriptural models tenaciously. Following this approach, Clarke may have implied such an interpretation in fact without the expected positive claim because it is through the local church where Jesus's commission is obeyed. Further Clarke allowed for such an uninterrupted break of a faithful line of Christians because he believed that the Holy Spirit aided Christ's disciples to continue and perpetuate the faith. Such a suggestion appeared in Clarke's remark, "that he intended the same unto other visible disciples that should love him and keep his commandments unto the end of the world."[45]

BAPTIST ANTIQUITY

Harking back to the New Testament order, Clarke perceived the Gospel successors as those who kept the biblical faith and not ones who have been identified only by name. Like their ancient heritage from the British Lollards of the fourteenth-sixteenth centuries, the Waldenses of the ninth-fifteenth centuries, and Paulician forefathers of earlier centuries, Clarke believed in and practiced missionary work. His method of spreading the "Good News" was through preaching and teaching. He was persuaded that coercion could not accomplish what the power of the gospel through preaching could. People voluntarily receive the message of God, Clarke argued, when the heart is awakened by the quickening Spirit of God. To him, therefore, if this method failed to accomplish the intended result, then no power or force of men on earth could perform the task.

DIFFERENT VIEWS ON THE NATURE OF A CHURCH

A sister church to the one Clarke pastored at Newport seemed to have expressed a broader view on the nature of a New Testament church, and there existed some difference within the Particular Baptists on the doctrine of last things. Otherwise there was remarkable agreement among the Regular Baptists at large. Fortunately excellent help is provided here by other contemporary records of the Baptists. The First Baptist Church of Boston from its inception in 1665 kept the most adequate records of any of the earlier Baptist churches in the New World. These records shed considerable light on understanding the nature of the church as viewed by these early Baptists. This First Baptist Church was in close fellowship with Clarke and his brethren at Newport; regular correspondence passed between them.

Author and pastor Nathan E. Wood edited an early letter of apology by John Russell called "Russell's Narrative," which was printed in 1680. In the Narrative, Elder Russell described in various terms the nature of a group of disciples who choose to assemble for worship as a church. Such services were conducted simply, there being no demanding echelon levels of clergy on the Lord's Day (Sunday) worship service. Observed by the church were two ordinances: baptism and the Lord's Supper; both were simple, unadorned ceremonies. Moreover the services included Scripture reading, prayer, preaching, an offering, and the exhortation of one another from Scripture. Following these, the Lord's Supper was observed in symbolic fashion as a memorial of Christ's redemption at Calvary.

In all of the earliest printed minutes and correspondences relating to the titles of Baptist churches, they are cited variously as "A body by themselves," "a particular body, or Church,...a visible Church of Christ,...being an entire Church, and body by ourselves..."[46] In a letter to Samuel Hubbard of the Newport church on January 9, 1674, as recorded by author Wood, the name "Church of the baptized" is cited.[47]

These early Baptists held that scripturally, any group of baptized believers could voluntarily assemble and organize themselves into a church, elect their own officers, and then observe the Lord's Supper in church capacity. Common officers during the seventeenth-nineteenth centuries consisted of a pastor, teaching Elder, ruling Elder—when available—and deacons. The role of a ruling Elder was that of visiting the distressed and sick, keeping a close watch and care over the church, and even rebuking and administering discipline within the body.[48] The pastor, of course, was the undershepherd and coordinator of the flock. Such an assembly also ordained deacons as needed to complete their core staff of church officers and teachers.[49]

The Baptist congregation at Boston observed the Lord's Supper once a month,[50] and like the church at Newport—along with others of like faith and order—they admitted only baptized believers to their communion. As their records reveal, only "visible Saints" are to be baptized, but "it is not Baptism that can make Saints," they stated.[51] Their simple order and practices were remarkably in harmony with all of those Baptist groups among the Particular Baptist persuasion, yet there were some points of difference in their beliefs.

CHURCH AND STATE ISSUE

A point of sharp difference emerged among some of them regarding how they viewed the Puritan churches. At least certain ministers of the Boston congregation did not share Clarke's sentiments that the Puritan congregations were not churches but were alien to Christ. Both Governor Endicott and Puritan church teacher Cobbet, an antagonist of Clarke's, rose up in defiance against the Baptist objection and censure of infant baptism because the Puritans tied in infant baptism with their church/state theocracy. As it happened, Cobbet interpreted the Baptist stand against their practice as stripping them of any church ministry whatsoever. Author Wood recorded Cobbet's defiance as follows:

> And I add, that theyr very principle of makeing infant Baptisme a nullity, it doth make at once, all our churches, & our religious, Civill state and polity, and all the officers & members thereof to be unbaptized & to bee no Christians, & so our Churches to bee no churches: & so we have no regular power to choose Deputies for any Generall Courts, nor to chuse any Magistrates.[52]

Wood confessed to this inexorable logic, and he viewed the abandonment of infant baptism as "the utter destruction of the compact between Church and State." It appears obvious from Cobbet's view that the Puritans did not separate their religious practices and beliefs from their government rule. According to Wood, Elder Russell did not disallow the Puritan churches in the way Cobbet deduced, although Clarke did. Russell said, "We have owned them as Churches of Christ…though they may be defective in some things."[53]

Of course it seems apparent that the Baptists in Newport never shared Elder Russell's concession on this point. Yet the author did not find a record that showed where a breach of fellowship occurred between the two churches over this belief. The issue, in fact, appears to have been resolved in both congregations by mutually refusing to fellowship in any way with the Puritans and other non-Baptists. When one from other than a Baptist church united with the Baptists, the one was baptized as though the one had never been baptized before. Moreover no letters of a church nature were ever exchanged between the Baptists and Puritans during this period of the seventeenth century.

By and large, Baptist churches and ministers were separate from state or governmental alliances. In this they were aligned with sixteenth-century continental Anabaptism. While the Baptists of Rhode Island obeyed the laws of the land, their religious way was not tied to the secular power as were those of the other twelve colonies.

The two arms of society the secular and ecclesiastical, Clarke believed, were two distinct and separate powers of rule, one temporal and the other spiritual. To him these two should and could function without infringing on each other's domain, which Clarke demonstrated in a very real and workable manner. Yet to him, there was not the so-called "invisible wall of church and state separation," as it is argued by many today. As a matter of fact, some well-known seventeenth-century Baptists held offices in the government such as Henry Jessey, William Kiffin and others.

Thus like the Anabaptist belief and basic to Clarke's theology—relative to the propagation of the Christian faith—Clarke adhered to the command of the Great Commission by following the "first Commissioners of Christ Jesus." These teachings, he contended, command the duly baptized candidate to be "so visibly planted into Christ…and having so received him, should walk in him."[54] Any deviation from this express command, as Clarke considered it, was denounced as heresy and apostasy.

The orderly walk for all duly-made disciples was of equal importance to Clarke. This, he noted, began only after uniting in fellowship with other baptized ones: "The first thing whereof as touching order was, to be added or joined one to another in the fellowship of the Gospel by a mutual professed subjection to the Scepter of Christ." This joining he explained as uniting with "a company" of baptized redeemed ones who are to avoid "worldly vanities, and worldly worships." Further this company of baptized ones he called the "Church of Christ," the same company that the Bible calls "the household of faith."[55]

ORDER OF A LOCAL CHURCH BODY

A visible, local type of congregation of baptized believers was the only kind that Clarke addressed. This company of faithful as "spiritual societies," which he called them in citing the churches of Galatia, consisted of both men and women, but the women were silent in the church. Contrary to what some unwitting writers have claimed, among Regular Baptists women did not preach or even deliver public addresses in church worship services. This appears evident from Clarke's statement that "women are directed to ask their husbands at home if they will learn." His conviction was based on the Apostle Paul's charge: "It is a shame for them to speak in the Church."[56]

The nature of this spiritual assembly, the church, is that of a holy brotherhood, according to Clarke. In this spiritual bond, he perceived the body as a Holy Spirit energized unit of Christian service. As he phrased it,

I believe that as God prepared a begetting ministry, even so doth he also prepare a feeding ministry in the church, where a called people out of the world, by the word and Spirit of the Lord, assembling of themselves together in a holy brotherhood, continuing in the apostles' doctrine, fellowship, breaking bread and prayer.[57]

Further, as an assembly thus voluntarily gathered, the group when guided by the Holy Spirit chose their own officers. Clarke's notation on this appeared in his creed, as follows:

I believe such a church ought to wait for the Holy Spirit of promise, on whom it may fall, and to choose out among themselves either pastor, teacher, or elders to rule, or deacons to serve the table, that others may give themselves to the word and prayer, and to keep them close to the Lord, and their fellowship clear and distinct, not to have fellowship with the unfruitful works of darkness, but rather to reprove them.[58]

Unlike other details in Clarke's writings, the doctrine of the Lord's Supper is given little attention. To Clarke its design was only a symbolic reminder to its participants of the death of Christ for sins. In keeping with his theological posture, however, the observance of the Supper was restricted to those who were baptized by immersion as believers and in regular fellowship with the congregation observing the ceremony.[59]

Since Clarke gave little attention to the Lord's Supper, it would seem that his uncompromising attitude toward a violation of the symbolic application of the ordinance of baptism would leave little room to doubt but that he held the same undaunted respect toward the observance of the symbol of the Supper. It would then seem to follow that a violation of the symbol would constitute a perversion of its intended focus, namely the broken body and shed blood of Christ for sin.

While no mention was made of how often the Lord's Supper was observed, the church met regularly on the first day of the week.[60]

CLARKE'S ESCHATOLOGY: DOCTRINE OF LAST THINGS

Clarke's Eschatology was chiliastic—that is, he believed in a form of the pre-millennial coming of Christ in His second advent. This belief set forth the notion that a 1,000-year reign on earth would begin when Christ returned the second time. In this doctrine Clarke and his brethren were out of step with much of contemporary theology and a number of their contemporary Baptist brethren. Some of the British Baptists, especially General Baptists, were involved in the Fifth Monarchist movement, which espoused a form of Post-Millennialism. This movement led by Venner in 1658, believed that Jesus Christ would return and set up His headquarters in London for the 1,000-year reign, but only after peace on earth was realized. Of course Clarke and his English Baptist associates such as William Kiffin—pastor of the Devonshire Square Baptist Church in London—and other Particular Baptists were not involved in the political insurrection as some others were, especially among the General Baptists.[61]

To Clarke the Kingdom would not be ushered in by mankind through social or political reforms but only by Christ when He returns to earth at His second coming (parousia). In fact, when this event occurs, as Clarke expressed it, Christ will descend from Heaven "in the form of a King with his glorious Kingdom, according to promise."[62] Only at this time will the saints of God reign with Christ in His millennial Kingdom.[63] During this future world-saving event, the righteous faithful, Clarke maintained, will be rewarded by certain vested priorities. Indeed, in his discussion of Matthew 25, Clarke posited that the Lord will then say: "Have thou Authority (in my Kingdom) over ten cities."[64]

The details of Clarke's belief regarding the second coming are scattered, very general and—to a large degree—allegorical. Like many other writers of that period, Clarke spiritualized considerably on the eschatology of the book of Revelation or Apocalypse. Yet he believed in the return of Israel and Judah to their ancient homeland before this Second Advent so that they, along with those in Christ—both dead (who will be raised) and living at His coming—"may reign with him a thousand years, according to the Scripture."[65]

MISSIONARY VIEWS

Baptists, as revealed through Clarke's faith, became known by their evangelistic or missionary efforts. A mission spirit and its emerging widespread practice were obviously a challenge to the Baptist way from its earliest New England inception. This became evidenced by the long and controversial missionary crusade waged by Clarke and Mark Lucar at Seekonk in 1649. The repercussions from this venture were shocking, to say the least, but the overall effect was gratifying to the Baptists. Very soon Baptists appeared in numbers, and their impact ranged far and wide, being felt throughout all New England in record time.[66]

VOLUNTARY WORSHIP

The Baptist religious persuasion was in stark contrast to that of the Bay area at large. Aside from the difference in church order, the Baptist way of maintaining their faith was strictly voluntary whereas the Puritan congregational order assumed a form of secular coercion that, in turn, clashed with other religious persuasions. To be sure, one had no choice whether to join one of the Bay churches; that was made a colonial law, as Clarke and others learned.

As a voluntarily assembled group of baptized believers, every member of a Baptist church was free to speak as the Holy Spirit led such a one. The church as an assembly of such believers, in fact, was under the direct leadership of the Holy Spirit, Clarke argued, and each member in turn so conducted oneself under the submission of the Spirit. As Clarke expressed it in Article 31 of his creed: "I believe the church of Christ, or this company gathered, are bound to wait on the Lord for the Spirit to help them, and have liberty, and are under duty, that they may prophesy one by one."[67]

Clarke held to no manner of forced worship. Like Williams of Providence, Clarke was very sensitive to the issue and vehemently opposed the control of religious consciences. He was very repetitious on this subject, of course, and the following words seem to highlight the central concern and motif of his arguments concerning the freedom of religious consciences:

> This outward forcing men in the worship of God, is the ready way to make men dissemblers and hypocrites before God, and men which wise men abhor...for if they be spirituall, true, and willing worshippers, such as the Father seeks for, then what need is there of a constraint or restraint? such are a law of life to themselves; but if they be not, then what make they there before him, who calls for the heart, and wisheth men to look to their spirits, for he is a Spirit, and will be sanctified of all those that draw neer unto him?...If Christ Iesus the Lord hath expressly forbidden his mans conscience, or his outward man against his understanding and conscience, in things appertaining to God, although his understanding and conscience, be cleerly discerned to be erronious and evil, then can no servant of Christ Jesus have any liberty, much less authority, from him so to practice...[68]

Clarke's prolific arguments against forced worship are presented in eight lengthy propositions. His polemics are as clear and pointed as those credited to Roger Williams, but which one affected the other is uncertain. In order to understand and fully appreciate Clarke's motives and suppositions on this issue, a close reading of his entire treatise becomes necessary.[69]

Thus Clarke communicated his convictions with unflagging zeal. To him they were central to a well-ordered life and peaceful existence in society. They were so crucial to him—and he felt to mankind in general also—that he sought to spread his faith to all around him. In doctrinal matters, Clarke was unwavering. All churches and religious persons not in sympathy with his beliefs, Clarke never fellowshipped within church capacity. Of course he did believe such persons may be in the family of God by virtue of a right relationship to Christ. But on church order, such ones may be out of step with the Word of God.

Clarke's religious position, it would seem, did not affect Clarke's social and political relationships. In the social and political arenas, he proved to be a man of great merit. He pioneered in American medicine. He served his community as a distinguished medical doctor, having extracted the first Hydatidiform Mole in the New World. In the field of law and political science, Dr. Clarke was well in advance of his age. He pioneered in the early formation of Rhode Island, having written and codified many of its early laws. His "lively experiment" in democracy has become so well entrenched that today this form of government has affected most all nations of the world in one way or another.

As a government "of the people, by the people, and for the people," to borrow from a great President of the United States, Abraham Lincoln, its guarantees of freedom, especially religious freedom, were written into the United States constitution by way of the First Amendment and treasured by a vast majority of the American people. To many this was Dr. John Clarke's greatest contribution to America because it is basic to a free society. As it happened, Clarke wrote most or all of the charter. Almost all of his letters and correspondences to the British King, which contained his desires and intents for Rhode Island, were incorporated in the document. So he patiently lobbied for a charter of democracy for the thirteenth colony—Rhode Island—during the stormy political period of Great Britain from 1651 to 1663.

CHAPTER XI ENDNOTES

1. Ephesians 3:15, KJV.

2. Clarke and Obadiah Holmes, Articles of Faith, Article 1, Backus, *History of the Baptists*, I:206–209. Hereafter cited as Clarke, Articles. Holmes penned these beliefs to his brother Robert, who lived in the parish of Manchester, Lancashire, England as the earliest formal creed of Clarke and the Newport congregation. Backus copied them from the Holmes manuscript of 1675; they are basically in harmony with the Particular Baptists of London. Due to the length of Article 1, it is printed in Appendix B *in toto*.

3. Clarke, "To the true Christian Reader," *Ill Newes*, pp. 18–22.

4. Clarke, "To the Right Honorable the House of Parliament," *Ill Newes*, pp. 3–9. Hereafter cited as Clarke, "Epistle Dedicatory."

5. Clarke, *Ill Newes*, pp. 40–48.

6. Clarke, Article 13.

7. Ibid., Article 2.

8. Clarke, *Ill Newes*, p. 42.

9. Ibid., pp. 43–44; Articles 8, 9.

10. Clarke, Articles, 2, 3, 22, 23.

11. Ibid., Articles 10, 11, 12.

12. Clarke, *Ill Newes*, p. 58.

13. Ibid., p. 12; Article 3.
    To the Anabaptist, Christ's death restored every person to the innocent state of Adam before Adam disobeyed God. Thus persons are born without a chargeable sin nature. But when a person becomes aware of sin that person must either accept Christ as Savior or perish. Therefore, infants are not accountable for sin effectually, only essentially.

14. Ibid., p. 47; Articles 34, 35.

15. Clarke, Articles 16, 24.

16. Clarke, *Ill Newes*, p. 14; cf. Ephesians 6:17.

17. Clarke, Articles 6, 7, 16.

18. Clarke, *Ill Newes*, pp. 56, 57; Articles 8, 9, 15, 16–25, 33.

19. Clarke, Articles 26, 24, 22.

20. Ibid., 23, 26, 21.

21. Ibid., 28–32; cf. Appendix B. Hardshellism is another name for fatalism. It claims that all things that come to pass were predetermined and no amount of human interference will modify it.

22. Providence is very seldom cited and then the allusions are both confused and unclear; cf. Clarke, *Ill Newes*, pp. 45, 52. The term Regular Baptists did not appear until the 18th century; it denoted those Baptists who chose to follow the Phil. Assoc. Confession. Here Regular refers to the Particular Baptists.

23. Edwards, *Materials*, Vol. VI; In *Collections of the Rhode Island Historical Society*, 314. Olney ministered to the group at Providence after Williams left; Dexter was a printer who came to Providence in 1640; Tillingham was in business and went to Providence from Newport.

24. Clarke, "To the Mathatusets Colony in New-England," *Ill Newes*, pp. 12–15.

25. Ibid., p. 32. The same charge was brought against Holmes; ibid., p. 44.

26. Ibid., pp. 36, 82–85; Articles 28, 32.

27. Ibid., pp. 36, 85.

28. Ibid., p. 93.

29. Clarke, *Ill Newes*, p. 80.

30. Ibid., pp. 82–85.

31. Ibid, pp. 50, 85.

32. Ibid., p. 83; Article 32.

33. Clarke, *Ill Newes*, pp. 82–85.

34. Ibid., pp. 82–84, 90, 93.

35. Ibid., p. 85.

36. William T. David, ed. *Bradford's History of Plymouth Plantation 1606–1646* (New York: Barnes & Noble, n.d.), pp. 362–63. The following is the account in Bradford's History:
> ...Mr. Charles Chansey, a reverend, godly, and very larned man, intending upon triall to chose him pastor of the church hear...But ther fell out some difference aboute baptizing, he holding it ought only to be by diping, and putting the whole body under water, and that sprinkling was unlawfull, but in this could countrie not so conveniente...but they were willing to yeeld to him as far as they could, and to the utmost; and were contented to suffer him to practise as he was perswaded; and when he came to minister that ordinance, he might so doe it to any that did desire it in that way, provided he could peacably suffer Mr. Reinor, and such as desired to have theirs otherwise baptised by him, by sprinkling or powering on of water upon them; so as ther might be no disturbance in the church hereaboute. But he said he could not yeeld herunto...so Mr. Chansey, having been the most parte of 3. years here, removed him selfe to Sityate, wher he now remaines a minister to the church ther.

37. Lechford, *Plain Dealing*; cf. Chapter VII, note 29.

38. Clarke, *Ill Newes*, p. 84. The Scriptures include the following: Matt 28:19, 20; Mark 16:15, 16; Acts 2:38, 41; 8:36, 38; 10:47, 48; Gal. 1:7, 8; Jude 3; II Tim. 2:2; Col. 2:5, 6; Heb. 12:25; Rev. 2:25; 3:11; 22:14.

39. Ibid., p. 86.

40. Ibid., p. 91.

41 Ibid., pp. 85–86; 90.

42. Ibid.

43. Ibid., pp. 11–15, 30–32, 44, *et passim*. The question of whether God gives the church or the ministers such authority to baptize was discussed by Philadelphia Association but never resolved; most churches hold to church authority to baptize.

44. Ibid., p. 86.

45. Ibid., p. 92.

46. Wood, *History of the First Baptist Church of Boston*, pp. 129, 152, 164.

47. Ibid., p. 121.

48. Ibid., p. 133.

49. Ibid., pp. 193–94.

50. Ibid., p. 136.

51. Ibid., pp. 170–71.

52. Ibid., pp. 173–74. The name Anabaptist was cited over 200 years before the Zurich movement of 1525. The ancient people called Anabaptists believed that infant baptism originated claiming it as a means of removing Original Sin. They denied that the doctrine of Original Sin originated in order to justify infant baptism. Cf. Thieleman Jansz van Braght, ed. *The Bloody Theater or Martyrs Mirror of the Defenseless Christians*, trans. Joseph F. Sohm (Scottdale, Pennsylvania: Herald Press, 1972), p. 322, col. 2; *et passim*.

53. Ibid., pp. 173–74, 171, 322.

54. Clarke, *Ill Newes*, p. 90.

55. Ibid.

56. Ibid., pp. 99, 95.

57. Clarke, Article 29.

58. Ibid., 30, 31.

59. Clarke, *Ill Newes*, p. 90.

60. Ibid., p. 47.

61. Most of the Particular Baptists held to the Pre-millennial doctrine—that is, Christ would return before His literal kingdom of a 1,000-year reign on earth would be established, according to author's research. William Kiffin wrote a book about the kingdom entitled: *A glimpse of Sions Glory*...:(London: Printed for William Larnar, 1641). The author read this book while at the Angus Library, Regent's Park College, Oxford Univ. Oxford, England in 1975.

62. Clarke, *Ill Newes*, p. 91; cf. also pp. 36, 78–79; 91, 94–95, 101. In Article 33, Clarke implies only those in Christ—both dead and living—will be changed at Christ's first appearing.

63. Ibid., p. 101; Article 33.

64. Ibid., p. 95.

65. Clarke, Article 33.

66. Sprague, *Annals of the American Baptist Pulpit*, vol. VI:*passim*.

67. Clarke, Article 31.

68. Clarke, *Ill Newes*, pp. 104–105.

69. Ibid., cf. pp. 98–113.

Appendix A
Outline Assessment of John Clarke 1609–1676

(1) Physician
In Rhode Island and England
Physician to Ann Marbury Hutchinson in 1638
Medical contributions honored by New England Journal of Medicine

(2) Minister
Baptist church organizer, missionary, theologian, and pastor

(3) Pioneer and Colonizer
Appointed to lead expedition to search out land for new settlement
In first Rhode Island group to procure land; drew up land sale contract
Helped colonize Rhode Island towns of Portsmouth and Newport
On committee to obtain patent from England in 1639 and again in 1642

(4) Statesman
Framed Portsmouth Compact of 1638—biblical guidelines from his Bible
Unification of towns in early Rhode Island
Rhode Island Commissioner in 1648
Rhode Island Colonial agent in London from 1651–1664
Obtained charter for Democracy in 1663
Representative in England on boundary disputes
Thrice Deputy-Governor of Rhode Island

(5) Attorney at Law
Drew up numerous contracts
codified laws of Rhode Island
Court Counselor in early Rhode Island colony of Jurisprudence
Lobbyist for Rhode Island colony in British Parliament
Legal Counselor (Barrister) out of Gray's Inn, London
Defense against Puritan Elders of Massachusetts in 1651
Attorney on Rhode Island boundary disputes

(6) Patriot
Labored for and achieved classic charter of government

Counsel sought in Indian relations in year of death; 1676, during King
Philip's War

(7) Author

Ill Newes from New England...
Bible *Concordance*
Principal tenets of Democratic Charter provisions
Ten typewritten-page of "Last Will and Testament"

(8) Scholar

In law, theology, medicine, languages, and political science

(9) Philosopher

On Church-State relations
On government, democratic process
Called philosopher and statesman by King Charles II of England
On political, religious, and social principles and rights

(10) Philanthropist

Bequeathed Trust Fund for needy children's education, out of which
grew the oldest trust company in the United States
Gave money and time to Rhode Island for Charter of Freedom
Bequeathed land for Newport Baptist Church property.

Appendix B
Articles of Faith by Obadiah Holmes and John Clarke

"The decree of God is that whereby God hath from eternity set down with himself whatsoever shall come to pass in time. Eph. i.2. All things with their causes, effects circumstances and manner of being, are decreed by God. Acts, ii.23...2 Acts, iv. 28. This decree is most wise; Rom. xi. 33; most just; Rom. ix. 13. 14; eternal; Eph. i. 4, 5; II Thes. ii. 13; necessary; Psa. xxxiii. 2, Prov. xix. 21; unchangeable; Heb. vi. 17; most free; Rom. ix. 13; and the cause of all good; Jam. i. 17; but not of any sin; I John, i.5. The special decree of God concerning angels and men is called predestination. Rom. viii. 30. Of the former, viz., angels, little is spoken of in the Holy Scripture; of the latter more is revealed, not unprofitable to be known. It may be defined, the wise, free, just, eternal and unchangeable sentence or decree of God, determining to create and govern man for his special glory, viz., the praise of his glorious mercy and justice; Rom. ix. 17, grace and mercy, choosing some men to faith, holiness and eternal life, for the praise of his glorious mercy; I Thes. I. 4, II Thes. ii. 13, Rom. viii. 29, 30. The cause which moved the Lord to elect them who are chosen, was none other but his mere good will and pleasure, Luke xii, 32. The end is the manifestation of the riches of his grace and mercy, ix. 23, Eph. i. 6. The sending of Christ, faith, holiness, and eternal life, are the effects of his love, by which he manifesteth the infinite riches of his grace. In the same order God doth execute this decree in time, he did decree it in his eternal counsel. I Thes. v. 9; II Thes. ii. 13. Sin is the effect of man's free will, and condemnation is an effect of justice inflicted upon man for sin and disobedience...A man in this life may be sure of this election, II Pet. i., 10, I Thes. i, 4; yea of his eternal happiness, ...but not of his eternal reprobation; for, he that is now profane, may be called hereafter.[3]

I believe there is one Essence or Being, even one God, who made heaven and earth, the waters, and all things therein contained, who governs all things by the word of his power, and hath appointed life and death to men, and bounded their habitations, whose providence extendeth to the least creature and actions.

2. I believe this God is Father to our Lord Jesus Christ; in a special understanding may be distinguished as Father, Son and Holy Spirit, and yet but one in Essence.

3. I believe that as God made the world, so by his word made he man in his own image without sin, and gave him a most excellent place and being, giving him commandment what he should do, and what he should forbear; but through the malice of Satan working with his wife was deceived; for she did eat, and gave her husband and he did eat, which was the first cause of the curse to him, and reached to all his posterity, by which came death natural, and death eternal.

4. I believe in this interim of time the Lord manifested his great love in that word, 'The seed of the woman shall break the head of the serpent,' but enmity was between the two seeds.

5. I believe that at that time and after time the Lord was worshipped by sacrifices, though darkly held forth to us.

6. I believe after that God in his own time chose a people to himself, and gave them his laws and statutes in a special manner, though he had always his chosen ones in every generation.

7. I believe with this people he made a choice covenant to be their God, and they to be his people; which covenant they brake though he was a Father to them, and was grieved for them, and yet did not only give them his laws, but sent his prophets early and late, but they would not hear; and in fullness of time sent his only Son; but as they had abused his prophets, so they killed his only Son.

8. I believe God in his Son made a new convent, a sure and everlasting covenant, not like that he made with Israel, of which Moses, that faithful servant, was mediator, but a covenant of grace and peace through his only Son, that whosoever believed in him should not perish, but have everlasting life.

9. I believe that all those that are in this covenant of grace, shall never fall away nor perish, but shall have life in the Prince of Life, the Lord Jesus Christ.

10. I believe no man can come to the Son but they that are drawn by the Father to the Son, and they that come, he in no wise will cast away.

11. I believe he came to call sinners to repentance, for the whole need him not, but they that are sick.

12. I believe that by the shedding of his precious blood is my redemption, and not mine only, but all that are or shall be saved.

13. I believe that as he was God so was he man, for he did not take the nature of angels, but the nature of Abraham.

14. I believe God hath laid the iniquity of all his elect and called ones, upon him.

15. I believe the Father is fully satisfied, and the debt is truly paid to the utmost farthing, and the poor sinner is quit, and set free from all sin past, present and to come.

16. I believe the Holy Scriptures which testify of Christ in dark shadows and types, and all that was written of Christ in the prophets and Psalms; and that he was born of a virgin at Bethlehem, and come to his own and they received him not.

17. I believe he was put to death and hanged upon a tree, called the cross, and was buried, and the third day rose again according to the Scriptures, and appeared to many.

18. I believe he ascended to his Father and sitteth at his right hand, having made request for his.

19. I believe that the Father's commandment and his declaration of him is to be observed, when the Father uttered that voice saying, 'This is my beloved Son in whom I am well pleased; hear ye him.'

20. I believe there is no salvation but by him alone; no other name under heaven by which man can be saved.

21. I believe he is sent unto the world, and to be published to all men; but some, yea, many reject the counsel of God against themselves.

22. I believe none have power to choose salvation, or to believe in Christ for life; it is only the gift of God.

23. I believe although God can bring men to Christ, and to cause them to believe in him for life, yet he hath appointed an ordinary way to effect that great work of faith, which is by means of sending a ministry into the world, to publish repentance to the sinner, and salvation, and that by Jesus Christ; and they that are faithful shall save their own souls and some that hear them.

24. I believe that they that are sent of God are not to deliver a mission of their own brain, but as it is in the Scripture of truth, for holy men wrote as they were inspired by the Holy Spirit.

25. I believe no man is to rush into the ministry without a special call from God, even as gospel ministers had of old, which was the call of the Holy Spirit, with some talent or talents to declare the counsel of God to poor sinners, declaring the grace of God through Jesus Christ,

even to those that are yet in the power of Satan; yea, to bring glad tidings by and from the Lord Jesus Christ.

26. I believe the precious gifts of the Spirit's teaching were procured by Christ's ascension and given to men for begetting of souls to the truth, and for establishment and consolation of those that are turned to the Lord; for none shall pluck them out of his Father's hand.

27. I believe this ministry is to go forth, and he that hath received grace with a talent or talents, as he hath received freely of the Lord, so he is freely to give, looking for nothing again but the promise of the Lord.

28. I believe none is to go forth but by commission, and carefully to observe the same according as Christ gave it forth without adding or diminishing; first to preach Christ, that is to make disciples, and then to baptize them, but not to baptize them before they believe; and then to teach them what Christ commanded them. For as the Father had his order in the former dispensation, so hath the Son. In former times the Lord spake in diverse ways and manners, but now hath he spoken by his Son.

29. I believe that as God prepared a begetting ministry, even so doth he also prepare a feeding ministry in the church, where a called people out of the world, by the word and Spirit of the Lord, assembling of themselves together in a holy brotherhood, continuing in the apostles' doctrine, fellowship, breaking bread and prayer.

30. I believe such a church ought to wait for the Holy Spirit of promise, on whom it may fall, and to choose out among themselves either pastor, teacher, or elders to rule, or deacons to serve the table, that others may give themselves to the word and prayer, and to keep them close to the Lord, and their fellowship clear and distinct, not to have fellowship with the unfruitful works of darkness, but rather to reprove them.

31. I believe the church of Christ, or this company gathered, are bound to wait on the Lord for the Spirit to help them, and have liberty, and are under duty, that they may prophesy one by one.

32. I believe that the true baptism of the gospel, is a visible believer with his own consent to be baptized in common water, by dying, or as it were drowning, to hold forth death, burial and resurrection, by a messenger of Jesus, into the name of the Father, Son, and Holy Spirit.

33. I believe the promise of the Father, concerning the return of Israel and Judah, and the coming of the Lord to raise up the dead in Christ, and to change them that are alive, that they may reign with him a thousand years, according to the Scripture.

34. I believe the resurrection of the wicked to receive their just judgment, Go ye cursed to the devil and his angels forever.

35. I believe, as eternal judgment to the wicked, so I believe the glorious declaration of the Lord saying, Come ye blessed of my Father, enter into the joy of your Lord, which joy, eye hath not seen, ear hath not heard, neither can it enter into the heart of man to conceive the glory that God hath prepared for them that love and wait for his appearance; wherefore come Lord Jesus, come quickly!"

APPENDIX B ENDNOTES

1. These Articles were formerly in the Newport church records; they were transferred to the Backus Papers at Brown University. They now appear in Backus, *History of the Baptists*, I, 206f.

Elder Obadiah Holmes was educated at Oxford, and while Clarke was in England from 1651 to 1664, Holmes served as pastor of the first Newport congregation. When Clarke returned from England, he resumed the pastorate until his death on April 20, 1676, then Holmes was reelected and pastored the church until his death, which occurred on October 15, 1681.

2. These are Holmes's ellipses throughout the Articles of Faith.

Appendix C

Dr. Clarke's sermon preached at William Witter's home in Lynn, Massachusetts, in 1651, when Clarke was arrested by Puritan magistrates. It was an expository message from Rev. 6.[1]

"The opening of ye first seal, showeth by ye going forth of ye white horse ye powerful conquest made by ye glorious gospel of Christ in ye days of X [Christ] and his apostles, ye weapons of their warfare not being carnal, but might thro God to ye pulling down of strongholds to ye obedience of Christ, this victory and ye affects of it were famous for 2 or 300 years after X.

Ye 2d seal by ye coming forth of ye red horse, showeth ye bloody wars that arose in ye earth and chiefly at Jerusalem, ye next generation following and ye dreadful persecution of ye saints foretold by X Matt. 24, and also to his faithful church of Smyrna in chap. 2, ye shall have tribulation 10 days, meaning 10 reigns of cruelty.

Ye 3d showeth by ye black horse and his rider with ye balance in his hand, ye coming forth of grievous wolves foretold of, yt would make merchandize of ye word, seeking their gain from their (every) quarter and greedy of filthy (lucre), contrary to X and his apostles' commands and examples, then begun and still continued by pretended ministers even to this day and darkness of these times.

Ye opening of ye fourth seal under ye pale horse and his rider, wh was death and hell following, showing the dead and woful condition ye professors of ye gospel were now come into, as ye word mentioned chapt. 16, and 2d angel poured out his veyal on ye sea, and it became as ye blood of a dead man, and every living soul died in ye sea, the bottomless pit now being begun to be opened and ye smoke darkening ye sun and air.

Ye 5th seal showeth ye bloody work of ye scarlet coloured beast and of the whore of Babylon yt was drunken with ye blood of ye saints and martyrs of X, whose blood cryeth for vengeance agt their abomination of desolation.

Ye 6th seal showeth ye ruin and desolation of ye churches' enemies after their iniquity is come to ye full, their sun, in Wh they so gloried, should be black like sackcloth of hair, and their moon, stars, and all ye host of their heaven, their greater and lesser lights, shall flee as a scroll, by reason of ye earthquakes and shaking yt shall fall upon yt wicked state, and all ye supporters thereof: when ye Lord shall arise to shake terribly ye earth, Isa. 2, and this concurs with ye pouring out ye vials of wrath. Chapt. 16.

The opening of ye 7th seal, showeth ye saints ye rest promised after their long and great sufferings of tribulation, according to yt (word) of St. Paul of ye Thessalonians, (tribulation) to ym yt trouble you, and to you who are troubled rest with us; when ye Lord shall be revealed from heaven with his mighty angels in flaming fire, There is silence in heaven. Rest and quietness after so many exercises. Then is ye Lamb's book of life opened. Rev. 6."

1. * Copied from Comer, *Diary*, pp. 74–75; ye means the, and there are several abbreviations in the sermon such as "yt" which means "yet" and "ym" which means "you who."

Appendix D
John Clarke on Baptism

Clarke assigned nine biblical reasons why he believed that dipping was the only acceptable mode given in the Bible. To him this mode must be practiced in order to meet the Lord's command to propagate the Gospel order. They are given as follows from Clarke's book *Ill Newes…*:

1. The etymology of the English word for baptize means exclusively to dip or immerse. Clarke gave the illustration of King Naaman in II Kings 5;14 and the King's reluctance to respond to the prophet's command to dip himself in the River Jordan; ultimately, however, the king obeyed the prophet and was healed (p. 82).

2. On the use of the preposition in connection with water and agent, Clarke cited scriptures to substantiate his claim such as Mark 1:8, where the preposition for "in" is translated "with"; other places it is translated correctly; cf. Mark 1:5 and 16; I Cor. 10:2 "baptized in the cloud and in the Sea"; "in the Spirit on the Lords day," Rev. 1:10; in particular, Mark 1:8; "…he shall baptize you [in] the Holy Ghost," not "with," and numerous other places (p. 82).

Most importantly, to illustrate Clarke's meaning and mode of baptizing, he used such metaphors as a drowning, planting, overwhelming, burying, and plunging.

3. The use of the word baptize in scriptural illustrations such as the emblem among the Israelites when they "passed through the midst of the red…Sea on dry land…" I Cor. 10:1, 2 (pp. 82–83)

4. The manner of its execution: a person is put into and brought out of the water, exemplified by Philip and the Eunich, Acts 8:38, 39 (p. 83).

5. Clarke gave as an illustration John the Baptist and "much water," Luke 3:2, 3; John 3:23 (p. 83)

6. Further emblems and resemblances:
   Visibly put on Christ and visibly planted into His death, Gal. 3:27; Rom. 8:2, 3; 5:7; 8:11; I Cor. 15:29 (p. 84)

7. The symbols—burial of "old man," "former lusts and conversation" (p. 84).

8. The symbol of one's open declaration of visibly holding forth the resurrection of both Christ and the hope of a future believer's experience (pp. 84–85).

9. As a commandment of Christ—one is not faithfully following Christ except one obeys this form of dipping or immersing Mt. 28:19; Mk. 16:15–16; Acts 2:38, 41; 8:36, 38; 10:47, 48; Gal. 1:7–8; Jude 3: II Tim. 2:2; Col. 2:5–6; Heb. 12:25; Rev. 2:25, 22; 14:19.